# OCTAVIO PAZ

## Selected Poems

Also by Octavio Paz

*Configurations*
*Early Poems 1935–1955*
*Eagle or Sun?*
*A Draft of Shadows*

# OCTAVIO PAZ

## Selected Poems

Edited by **ELIOT WEINBERGER**

Translations from the Spanish by G. AROUL,
ELIZABETH BISHOP, PAUL BLACKBURN, LYSANDER KEMP,
DENISE LEVERTOV, MURIEL RUKEYSER, MARK STRAND,
CHARLES TOMLINSON, WILLIAM CARLOS WILLIAMS,
MONIQUE FONG WUST, and the editor

A NEW DIRECTIONS BOOK

The Spanish texts from which the translations in this volume were made are included in
Octavio Paz's *Poemas (1935-1975)* (Copyright © 1979 by Octavio Paz), Edition © 1979
Editorial Seix Barral, S. A. Most of the translations have been selected from *Con-
figurations* (1971), *Early Poems 1935-1955* (1973), *Eagle or Sun?* (1976), and *A Draft of
Shadows* (1979), all published by New Directions Publishing Corporation.

Manufactured in the United States of America
First published clothbound and as New Directions Paperback 574 in 1984
Published simultaneously in Canada by George J. McLeod, Ltd., Toronto

**Library of Congress Cataloging in Publication Data**
Paz, Octavio, 1914-
    Selected poems.
    (A New Directions Book)
    1. Paz, Octavio, 1914-        —Translations, English.
I. Weinberger, Eliot.   II. Aroul, G.   III. Title.
PQ7297.P285A29   1984        861        84-9856
ISBN 0-8112-0903-2
ISBN 0-8112-0899-0 (pbk.)

New Directions Books are published for James Laughlin
by New Directions Publishing Corporation,
80 Eighth Avenue, New York 10011

# Contents

Introduction     ix

*from* BAJO TU CLARA SOMBRA/"UNDER YOUR CLEAR SHADOW"
(1935-1944)
The bird     1
Two bodies     2
Poet's epitaph     2

*from* CALAMIDADES Y MILAGROS/"CALAMITIES AND MIRACLES"
(1937-1947)
The street     2

*from* SEMILLAS PARA UN HIMNO/"SEEDS FOR A PSALM"
(1943-1955)
"The hand of day opens"     3
Fable     3
Native stone     4
Object lesson     5
In Uxmal     7
Riprap     8

*from* ¿AGUILA O SOL?/"EAGLE OR SUN?" (1949-1950)
The poet's works III, IV, VII, XI, XII     10
The blue bouquet     12
Hurry     14
Plain     16
Capital     16
Obsidian butterfly     17
A poet     19
Huastec lady     19
Toward the poem     20

*from* LA ESTACION VIOLENTA/"THE VIOLENT SEASON" (1948-1957)
Hymn among the ruins     22
Is there no way out?     24

The river    27
Sun stone    29

*from* DIAS HABILES/"LAWFUL DAYS" (1958–1961)
Dawn    46
Here    46
Landscape    46
Certainty    47

*from* SALAMANDRA/"SALAMANDER" (1958–1961)
Touch    48
Duration    48
Last dawn    49
Salamander    50

*from* LADERA ESTE/"EAST SLOPE" (1962–1968)
Happiness in Herat    55
Apparition    57
In the Lodi gardens    57
The other    58
Vrindaban    58
Village    63
Daybreak    63
Nightfall    64
On reading John Cage    64
Writing    67
Concord    68
Exclamation    68

*from* HACIA EL COMIENZO/"TOWARD THE BEGINNING" (1964–1968)
Wind from all compass points    69
Madrigal    74
With eyes closed    75
Transit    75
Maithuna    76
The key of water    80
Sunday on the island of Elephanta    80

BLANCO (1966)
Blanco    82

*from* VUELTA/RETURN (1969–1975)
The grove     92
Immemorial landscape     93
Trowbridge Street     95
Objects and apparitions     97
Return     99
In the middle of this phrase . . .     103
The petrifying petrified     107
San Ildefonso nocturne     112

PASADO EN CLARO/"A DRAFT OF SHADOWS" (1974)
A draft of shadows     120

UNCOLLECTED POEMS (1976–1980)
Flame, speech     138
Sight, touch     139
Homage to Claudius Ptolemy     140
Stars and cricket     141
Wind and water and stone     141
Epitaph for no stone     142
This side     142

Author's notes     143

# Introduction

Mexico, perhaps more than China, is the Middle Kingdom. In the current political moment, its centrality lies on a north-south axis: for North Americans, as the relatively stable, partially friendly buffer state between "us" and the turmoil we misunderstand in Central America; for Mexicans, as a nation placed between the closing jaws of Northern imperialism and Southern revolt.

Historically, however, Mexico was a Middle Kingdom between the oceans, between East and West. Before the arrival of Cortez in 1519 the country was, it seems likely, the eastern edge of the transpacific cultural network—one that will never be fully known, but which is apparent in various artworks across the ocean: China, Japan, and India; Polynesia; Mexico, Peru, and Ecuador. With Cortez, of course, Mexico became the western end of the Spanish Empire, with a European language and religion, and with a government no more enlightened than its Aztec predecessor.

There is a navel (*xi*, in Nahuatl) in the middle of the word Mexico, and the navel of the Middle Kingdom was the city Tenochtitlán, today's Mexico City, built literally on the water, but facing no sea. It was the capital of an empire that radiated from its ring of volcanoes and pyramids: an expanding self-absorbed sun, devoted to feeding, with art and blood, the other, celestial sun.

Mexico—a xenophobe whom strangers won't leave alone—has been the center of a global mandala. It is this configuration that Octavio Paz has, in his life and in the work, traced to its furthest reaches. A great synthesizer, he has transformed the picture while simultaneously drawing his own self-portrait.

Born in a suburb of Mexico City in 1914, Paz began at the center and followed the Mexican mandala in three directions. East: as a young Marxist to the Spanish Civil War, and as a surrealist to Paris in the late 1940s. North: to San Francisco and New York during the Second World War, and in the 1970s to various American universities. West: to India and Japan in

1952, and as the Mexican ambassador to India from 1962 to 1968.

From the U.S. he gained a vision of overdevelopment and a view of his own country on the outskirts of history and the pathos of its nationalistic ardor. From Europe, the belief in poetry as "the secret religion of the modern age"; that the revolution of the word is the revolution of the world, and that both cannot exist without a revolution of the body: life as art, a return to the mythic lost unity of thought and body, man and nature, I and the other. From India, and his studies of Buddhism and Tantrism: the revelation of passion binding the world in illusion, and of passion as the liberator of the world: that in the moment of absolute integration, the world dissolves, "transparency is all that remains."

He is "a man in love with silence who can't stop talking," a restless mind, forever curious, in seemingly perpetual motion. There is something Aztec in this, despite that society's bloody singlemindedness and rigidity: In Nahuatl, the artist is *tlayolteuanni*, he who sees with his heart. Heart, *yollotl*, comes from the word movement, *ollin*. Living hearts were flung down the steps of the temples to feed the sun, to keep it moving. Time was a turning wheel, the familiar sun stone. For the Aztecs, the great terror was *stasis*—that the sun, time, the world would stop. Paz's mobility, though of course the product of an individual temperament, oddly fits the ancient scheme. Had he been born in Tenochtitlán, he might have been one of the poet-princes, but I imagine him as a *pochteca*, one of that mysterious band of pilgrims who wandered the empire in search of the "Land of the Sun."

Paz is generally read as Latin America's great surrealist poet—that is, as an exotic European. Yet he remains inherently Mexican, despite the fact that he has always been a cosmopolitan and never a regionalist or an indigenist. Like the hero of a Sufi parable, Paz traveled abroad to find what was always at home. He discovered synesthesia in Rimbaud's colored vowels, not in the Aztec "painted songs." He practiced dissolving the poet's ego through automatic writing and Japanese renga, but he came from a tradition that did not distinguish between poet and poem, where the poet declared, "God has sent me as a messenger./I am transformed into a poem."

x

The famous last line of "Hymn among the Ruins," "words that are flowers that are fruits that are acts," could have been written equally by a surrealist or by a member of the Aztec Brotherhood of poets. In the Nahuatl lyric form called *xopancuicatl*, a celebration of life and of cyclical time, the poet and the poem become a plant that grows with the poem; the plant becomes the fibers of the book in which the poem is painted; and the fibers of the book become the woven fiber of the mat, the symbol of worldly power and authority. Paz's preoccupation with pairs is also strangely Nahuatl: The Aztecs tended to describe the world by two aspects—poetry was "flower and song," fame "mist and smoke," pleasure "wind and heat"—"so that," as Angel Garibay writes, "through the union of these two will come a spark which will bring understanding."

Paz's great Tantric poem "Blanco" owes much to Mallarmé and to Pound's ideogrammic method—each image self-contained and discrete, understood (like the Chinese ideogram itself) only in relation to the other lines, written and unwritten; each a centripetal force drawing the other images and meanings toward it, an implosion that leads to the explosion of the poem. Yet "Blanco" was also designed as an Aztec book, a folded screen. Those screens of painted songs, images rather than what we would call writing, were "read" as mnemonic devices: the reader created the text, the text created itself, as "Blanco" with its variant readings intends.

The surrealists sought a way out of European rationalism and bourgeois capitalist values by recovering their own archaic history and by immersing themselves in the surviving indigenous cultures of the world. Paz, on a similar quest—to free himself from the straitjacket of ex-colonial provincialism, that child more orthodox than its parent—went to Europe to discover the other, heretical and subterranean, European tradition. It is an irony of the age: while Paz was writing on de Sade and Fourier, his friend the French poet Benjamin Peret was translating the Mayan *Book of the Chilam Balam of Chumayel*.

The surrealist motto—"liberty, love and poetry"—applies in varying degrees to most of the modernists of the first half of the century: women and men dedicated to the imagination, to social revolution, to the transformation of all the arts, to the integration of life and art. It seems incredible that that era has passed, that we have entered an age of specialized arts practitioners. Surely others will come, but at the moment Paz is among the last of the poets who drew their own maps of the world.

To read all that Paz has written would probably take a few years; to absorb it, a few lifetimes. The latest edition of his collected (not complete) poems alone fills some 700 pages. The selection here is largely derived from the four previous New Directions collections (*Early Poems, Configurations, Eagle or Sun?*, and *A Draft of Shadows*). Some of the translations, however, have never appeared in book form, including the long poem "Maithuna" and the present version of "Blanco." In most cases the poems chose themselves; Paz advised, but I must take the blame for the final selection.

For Paz, forever in motion, there is no definitive text. His tendency to revise his earlier work has even caused one academic critic to complain that Paz does not "respect" his own poems. The present translations have been revised from the earlier volumes to correspond to the most recent versions of the poems, those published in the Seix Barral edition *Poemas* (*1935-1975*). Where available, the original translators have made the revisions. With the translations of Paul Blackburn, Muriel Rukeyser, and William Carlos Williams, this was, sadly, not possible. I have, with reluctance, slightly altered some of their translations. These changes, signaled in the notes, involved deleting or adding a few lines or words. In no instance have I attempted to "improve" a translation, changing the English where the Spanish has not changed. Nevertheless, students of Blackburn, Rukeyser, and Williams should refer to the original translations, all of which remain in print.

Special thanks—again and always—to Peter Glassgold at New Directions and to Octavio Paz.

ELIOT WEINBERGER

# The bird

In transparent silence
day was resting:
the transparency of space
was silence's transparency.
Motionless light of the sky was soothing
the growth of the grass.
Small things of earth, among the stones,
under identical light, were stones
Time sated itself in the minute.
And in an absorbed stillness
noonday consumed itself.

And a bird sang, slender arrow.
The sky shivered a wounded silver breast,
the leaves moved,
and grass awoke.
And I knew that death was an arrow
let fly from an unknown hand
and in the flicker of an eye we die.

[M.R.]


# Two bodies

Two bodies face to face
are at times two waves
and night is an ocean.

Two bodies face to face
are at times two stones
and night a desert.

1

Two bodies face to face
are at times two roots
laced into night.

Two bodies face to face
are at times two knives
and night strikes sparks.

Two bodies face to face
are two stars falling
in an empty sky.

[M.R.]

# Poet's epitaph

He tried to sing, singing
not to remember
his true life of lies
and to remember
his lying life of truths.

[M.R.]

# The street

A long and silent street.
I walk in blackness and I stumble and fall
and rise, and I walk blind, my feet
stepping on silent stones and dry leaves.
Someone behind me also stepping on stones, leaves:
if I slow down, he slows;
if I run, he runs. I turn: nobody.

Everything dark and doorless.
Turning and turning among these corners
which lead forever to the street
where nobody waits for, nobody follows me,
where I pursue a man who stumbles
and rises and says when he sees me: nobody

[M.R.]

# (Untitled)

The hand of day opens
Three clouds
And these few words

[M.R.]

# Fable

Ages of fire and of air
Youth of water
From green to yellow
                From yellow to red
From dream to watching
                From desire to act
It was only one step and you took it so lightly
Insects were living jewels
The heat rested by the side of the pond
Rain was a willow with unpinned hair
A tree grew in the palm of your hand
And that tree laughed sang prophesied
Its divinations filled the air with wings
There were simple miracles called birds

Everything was for everyone
    Everyone was everything
There was only one huge word with no back to it
A word like a sun
One day it broke into tiny pieces
They were the words of the language we now speak
Pieces that will never come together
Broken mirrors where the world sees itself shattered

              [E.W.]


# Native stone

*For Roger Munier*


Light is laying waste the heavens
Droves of dominions in stampede
The eye retreats surrounded by mirrors

Landscapes enormous as insomnia
Stony ground of bone

Limitless autumn
Thirst lifts its invisible fountains
One last peppertree preaches in the desert

Close your eyes and hear the light singing:
Noon nests in your inner ear

Close your eyes and open them:
There is nobody not even yourself
Whatever is not stone is light

              [M.R.]

# Object lesson

1. ANIMATION

Over the bookcase
between a T'ang musician and a Oaxaca pitcher
incandescent, lively,
with glittering eyes of silver-paper
watching us come and go
the little sugar skull.


2. MASK OF TLALOC CARVED IN TRANSPARENT
QUARTZ

Petrified waters.
Old Tlaloc sleeps, within,
dreaming rainstorms.


3. THE SAME

Touched by light
quartz has become cascade.
Upon its waters floats the child, the god.


4. GOD WHO COMES FORTH FROM A CERAMIC ORCHID

Among clay petals
is born, smiling,
the human flower.


5. OLMEC GODDESS

The four cardinal points
are gathered in your navel.
In your womb the day is pounding, fully armed.

## 6. CALENDAR

Facing water, days of fire.
Facing fire, days of water.


## 7. XOCHIPILLI

In a day's tree
hang jade fruit,
fire and blood at night.


## 8. CROSS WITH SUN AND MOON PAINTED ON IT

Between the arms of this cross
two birds made their nest:
Adam, sun, and Eve, moon.


## 9. BOY AND TOP

Each time he spins it,
it lands, precisely,
at the center of the world.


## 10. OBJECTS

They live alongside us,
we do not know them, they do not know us.
But sometimes they speak with us.

[M.R.]

# In Uxmal

I. THE STONE OF THE DAYS

In the court, the sun stone, immobile;
above, the sun of fire and of time turns;
movement is sun and the sun is stone.

[E.W.]


2. NOON

Light unblinking,
time empty of minutes,
a bird stopped short in air.


3. LATER

Light flung down,
the pillars awake
and, without moving, dance.


4. FULL SUN

The time is transparent:
even if the bird is invisible,
let us see the color of his song.


5. RELIEFS

The rain, dancing, long-haired,
ankles slivered by lightning,
descends, to an accompaniment of drums:
the corn opens its eyes, and grows.

## 6. SERPENT CARVED ON A WALL

The wall in the sun breathes, shivers, ripples,
a live and tattooed fragment of the sky:
a man drinks sun and is water, is earth.
And over all that life the serpent
carrying a head between his jaws:
the gods drink blood, the gods eat man.

[M.R.]

# Riprap

### 1. FLOWER

Cry, barb, tooth, howls,
carnivorous nothingness, its turbulence,
all disappear before this simple flower.

### 2. SHE

Every night she goes down to the well
next morning reappearing
with a new reptile in her arms.

### 3. BIOGRAPHY

Not what he might have been:
but what he was.
And what he was is dead.

### 4. BELLS IN THE NIGHT

Waves of shadows, waves of blindness
on a forehead in flames:
water for my thought, drown it out!

8

## 5. AT THE DOOR

People, words, people.
I hesitated:
up there the moon, alone.


## 6. VISION

I saw myself when I shut my eyes:
space, space
where I am and am not.


## 7. LANDSCAPE

Insects endlessly busy,
horses the color of sun,
donkeys the color of cloud,
clouds, huge rocks that weigh nothing,
mountains like tilted skies,
a flock of trees drinking at the stream,
they are all there, delighted in being there,
and here we are not who are not,
eaten by fury, by hatred,
by love eaten, by death.

[M.R.]


## 8. ILLITERATE

I raised my face to the sky,
that huge stone of worn-out letters,
but the stars told me nothing.

[E.W.]

# *from* The poet's works

Everyone had left the house. Around eleven I noticed that I had smoked my last cigarette. Not wanting to expose myself to the wind and cold, I searched every cranny for a pack, without success. There was nothing to do but put on my overcoat and go downstairs (I live on the fifth floor). The street, a beautiful street with tall buildings of gray stone and two rows of bare chestnut trees, was deserted. I walked about three hundred yards against the freezing wind and yellowish fog only to find the shop closed. I turned toward a nearby café where I was sure to find a little warmth, some music, and above all cigarettes, the object of my search. I walked two more blocks, shivering, when suddenly I felt—no, I didn't feel it: it passed, quickly: the Word. The unexpectedness of the meeting paralyzed me for a second, long enough to give it time to return into the night. Recovered, I reached and grabbed it by the tips of its floating hair. I pulled desperately at those threads that stretched toward the infinite, telegraph wires that inevitably recede in a glimpsed landscape, a note that rises, tapers off, stretches out, stretches out . . . I was alone in the middle of the street, with a red feather between my livid hands.

IV

Lying on my bed, I crave the brute sleep, the mummy's sleep. I close my eyes and try not to hear that tapping in some corner of the room. "Silence is full of noise, and what you hear," I say to myself, "you do not truly hear. You hear the silence." And the tapping continues, louder each time: it is the sound of horses' hooves galloping on a field of stone; it is an ax that cannot fell a giant tree; a printing press printing a single immense verse made up of nothing but one syllable that rhymes with the beat of my heart; it is my heart that pounds the rock and covers it with a ragged coat of foam; it is the sea, the undertow of the chained sea that falls and rises, that rises and falls, that falls and rises; it is the great trowels of silence falling in the silence.

VII

I write on the glimmering table, my pen resting heavily on its chest that is almost living, that moans and remembers the forest of its birth. Great wings of black ink open. The lamp explodes and a cape of broken glass covers my words. A sharp sliver of light cuts off my right hand. I keep writing with this stump that sprouts shadows. Night enters the room, the opposite wall puckers its big stone lips, great blocks of air come between my pen and the paper. A simple monosyllable would be enough to make the world burst. But tonight there is no room for a single word more.

XI

It hovers, creeps in, comes close, withdraws, turns on tiptoe and, if I reach out my hand, disappears: a Word. I can only make out its proud crest: Cri. Cricket, Cripple, Crime, Crimea, Critic, Crisis, Criterion? A canoe sails from my forehead carrying a man armed with a spear. The light, fragile boat nimbly cuts the black waves, the swells of black blood in my temples. It moves further inward. The hunter-fisherman studies the shaded, cloudy mass of a horizon full of threats; he sinks his keen eyes into the rancorous foam, he perks his head and listens, he sniffs. At times a bright flash crosses the darkness, a green and scaly flutter. It is Cri, who leaps for a second into the air, breathes, and submerges again in the depths. The hunter blows the horn he carries strapped to his chest, but its mournful bellow is lost in the desert of water. There is no one on the great salt lake. And the rocky beach is far off, far off the faint lights from the huts of his companions. From time to time Cri reappears, shows his fatal fin, and sinks again. The oarsman, fascinated, follows him inward, each time further inward.

XII

After chopping off all the arms that reached out to me; after boarding up all the windows and doors; after filling all the pits with poisoned water; after building my house on the rock of a No inaccessible to flattery and fear; after cutting out my tongue and eating it; after hurling handfuls of silence and monosyllables of scorn at my loves; after forgetting my name and the name of my birthplace and the name of my race; after judging and sentencing myself to perpetual waiting and perpetual loneliness, I heard against the stones of my dungeon of syllogisms the humid, tender, insistent onset of spring.

[E.W.]

# The blue bouquet

I woke covered with sweat. Hot steam rose from the newly sprayed, red-brick pavement. A gray-winged butterfly, dazzled, circled the yellow light. I jumped from my hammock and crossed the room barefoot, careful not to step on some scorpion leaving his hideout for a bit of fresh air. I went to the little window and inhaled the country air. One could hear the breathing of the night, feminine, enormous. I returned to the center of the room, emptied water from a jar into a pewter basin, and wet my towel. I rubbed my chest and legs with the soaked cloth, dried myself a little, and, making sure that no bugs were hidden in the folds of my clothes, got dressed. I ran down the green stairway. At the door of the boardinghouse I bumped into the owner, a one-eyed taciturn fellow. Sitting on a wicker stool, he smoked, his eye half closed. In a hoarse voice, he asked:

"Where are you going?"

"To take a walk. It's too hot."

"Hmmm—everything's closed. And no streetlights around here. You'd better stay put."

I shrugged my shoulders, muttered "back soon," and plunged into the darkness. At first I couldn't see anything. I fumbled along the cobblestone street. I lit a cigarette. Suddenly the moon appeared from behind a black cloud, lighting a white wall that was crumbled in places. I stopped, blinded by such whiteness. Wind whistled slightly. I breathed the air of the tamarinds. The night hummed, full of leaves and insects.

12

Crickets bivouacked in the tall grass. I raised my head: up there the stars too had set up camp. I thought that the universe was a vast system of signs, a conversation between giant beings. My actions, the cricket's saw, the star's blink, were nothing but pauses and syllables, scattered phrases from that dialogue. What word could it be, of which I was only a syllable? Who speaks the word? To whom is it spoken? I threw my cigarette down on the sidewalk. Falling, it drew a shining curve, shooting out brief sparks like a tiny comet.

I walked a long time, slowly. I felt free, secure between the lips that were at that moment speaking me with such happiness. The night was a garden of eyes. As I crossed the street, I heard someone come out of a doorway. I turned around, but could not distinguish anything. I hurried on. A few moments later I heard the dull shuffle of sandals on the hot stone. I didn't want to turn around, although I felt the shadow getting closer with every step. I tried to run. I couldn't. Suddenly I stopped short. Before I could defend myself, I felt the point of a knife in my back, and a sweet voice:

"Don't move, mister, or I'll stick it in."

Without turning, I asked:

"What do you want?"

"Your eyes, mister," answered the soft, almost painful voice.

"My eyes? What do you want with my eyes? Look, I've got some money. Not much, but it's something. I'll give you everything I have if you let me go. Don't kill me."

"Don't be afraid, mister. I won't kill you. I'm only going to take your eyes."

"But why do you want my eyes?" I asked again.

"My girlfriend has this whim. She wants a bouquet of blue eyes. And around here they're hard to find."

"My eyes won't help you. They're brown, not blue."

"Don't try to fool me, mister. I know very well that yours are blue."

"Don't take the eyes of a fellow man. I'll give you something else."

"Don't play saint with me," he said harshly. "Turn around."

I turned. He was small and fragile. His palm sombrero covered half his face. In his right hand he held a field machete that shone in the moonlight.

13

"Let me see your face."

I struck a match and put it close to my face. The brightness made me squint. He opened my eyelids with a firm hand. He couldn't see very well. Standing on tiptoe, he stared at me intensely. The flame burned my fingers. I dropped it. A silent moment passed.

"Are you convinced now? They're not blue."

"Pretty clever, aren't you?" he answered. "Let's see. Light another one."

I struck another match, and put it near my eyes. Grabbing my sleeve, he ordered:

"Kneel down."

I knelt. With one hand he grabbed me by the hair, pulling my head back. He bent over me, curious and tense, while his machete slowly dropped until it grazed my eyelids. I closed my eyes.

"Keep them open," he ordered.

I opened my eyes. The blame burned my lashes. All of a sudden, he let me go.

"All right, they're not blue. Beat it."

He vanished. I leaned against the wall, my head in my hands. I pulled myself together. Stumbling, falling, trying to get up again, I ran for an hour through the deserted town. When I got to the plaza, I saw the owner of the boardinghouse, still sitting in front of the door. I went in without saying a word. The next day I left town.

[E.W.]

# Hurry

In spite of my torpor, my puffy eyes, my paunch, my appearance of having just left the cave, I never stop. I'm in a hurry. I've always been in a hurry. Day and night a bee buzzes in my brain. I jump from morning to night, sleep to waking, crowds to solitude, dawn to dusk. It's useless that each of the four seasons offers me its opulent table; useless the canary's morning flourish, the bed lovely as a river in summer, that adolescent and her tear, cut off at the end of autumn. In vain the noon sun and its crystal stem, the green leaves that filter it, the rocks that deny it, the shadows that it sculpts. All of these splendors just speed me up. I'm off and back, cough and hack, I spin in a grin, I stomp, I'm out, I'm in, I snoop, I hear a flute, I'm deep in my mind, I itch, opine, malign, I change my suit, I say adieu to what I was, I linger longer in what will be. Nothing stops me. I'm in a hurry, I'm going. Where? I don't know, know nothing—except that I'm not where I should be.

From when I first opened my eyes I've known that my place isn't here where I am, but where I'm not and never have been. Somewhere there's an empty place, and that emptiness will be filled with me and I'll sit in that hole that will senselessly teem with me, bubble with me until it turns into a fountain or a geyser. And then my emptiness, the emptiness of the me that I now am, will fill up with itself, full to the brim with being.

I'm in a hurry to be. I run behind myself, behind my place, behind my hole. Who has reserved this place for me? What is my fate's name? Who and what is that which moves me and who and what awaits my arrival to complete itself and to complete me? I don't know. I'm in a hurry. Though I don't move from my chair, though I don't get out of bed. Though I turn and turn in my cage. Nailed by a name, a gesture, a tic, I move and remove. This house, these friends, these countries, these hands, this mouth, these letters that form this image that without warning has come unstuck from I don't know where and has hit me across the chest, these are not my place. Neither this nor that is my place.

All that sustains me and that I sustain sustaining myself is a screen, a wall. My hurry leaps all. This body offers me its body, this sea pulls from its belly seven waves, seven nudes, seven whitecaps, seven smiles. I thank them and hurry off. Yes, the walk has been amusing, the conversation instructive, it's still early, the function isn't over, and in no way do I pretend to know the end. I'm sorry: I'm in a hurry. I'm anxious to get rid of my hurry. I'm in a hurry to go to bed and to get up without saying: good-by I'm in a hurry.

[E.W.]

# Plain

The anthill erupts. The open wound gushes, foams, expands, contracts. The sun at these times never stops pumping blood, temples swollen, face red. A boy—unaware that, in some corner of puberty, fevers and a problem of conscience await him—carefully places a small stone on the flayed mouth of the anthill. The sun buries its lances in the humps of the plain, crushing promontories of garbage. Splendor unsheathed, the reflections from an empty can—high on a pyramid of scraps—pierce every point of space. Treasure-hunting children and stray dogs poke in the yellow radiance of the rot. A thousand feet away, the church of San Lorenzo calls the twelve o'clock Mass. Inside, on the altar to the right, there is a saint painted blue and pink. From his left eye stream gray-winged insects that fly in a straight line to the dome and fall, turned to dust, a silent landslide of armor touched by the sun's hand. Whistles blow in the towers of the factories. Decapitated pricks. A bird, dressed in black, flies in circles and rests on the only living tree on the plain. And then . . . There is no then. I move forward, I pierce great rocks of years, great masses of compacted light, I go down into galleries of mines of sand, I travel corridors that close on themselves like granite lips. And I return to the plain, to the plain where it is always noon, where an identical sun shines fixedly on an unmoving landscape. And the ringing of the twelve bells never stops, nor the buzzing of the flies, nor the explosion of this minute that never passes, that only burns and never passes.

[E.W.]

# Capital

The screaming crest of dawn flames. First egg, first peck, decapitation and delight! Feathers fly, wings spread, sails swell, and wing-oars dip in the sunrise. Oh unreined light, first light rearing. Landslides of crystals burst from the mountain, tympanum-tamping timpani explode in my head.

Tastes nothing, scents nothing, the dawn, girl still nameless, faceless still. Arrives, moves forward, pauses, heads for the outskirts. Leaves a train of murmurs that open eyes. Becomes lost in herself. The day with its hasty foot crushes a small star.

[E.W.]

# Obsidian butterfly

They killed my brothers, my children, my uncles. On the banks of Lake Texcoco I began to weep. Whirlwinds of saltpeter rose from Peñon hill, gently picked me up, and left me in the courtyard of the Cathedral. I made myself so small and gray that many mistook me for a pile of dust. Yes I, mother of flint and star, I, bearer of the ray, am now but a blue feather that a bird loses in the brambles. Once, I would dance, my breasts high and turning, turning, turning until I became still, and then I would sprout leaves, flowers, fruit. The eagle throbbed in my belly. I was the mountain that creates you as it dreams, the house of fire, the primordial pot where man is cooked and becomes man. In the night of the decapitated words my sister and I, hand in hand, leapt and sang around the I, the only standing tower in the razed alphabet. I still remember my songs:

> *Light, headless light*
> *Golden-throated light*
> *Sings in the thicket green*

They told us: the straight path never leads to winter. And now my hands tremble, the words are caught in my throat. Give me a chair and a little sun.

In other times, every hour was born from the vapor of my breath, danced a while on the point of my dagger, and disappeared through the shining door of my hand mirror. I was the tattooed noon and naked midnight, the little jade insect that sings in the grass at dawn, and the clay nightingale that summons the dead. I bathed in the sun's waterfall, I bathed in myself, soaked in my own splendor. I was the flint that rips the storm clouds of night and opens the doors of the showers. I planted gardens of fire, gardens of blood, in the Southern sky. Its coral branches still graze the foreheads of lovers. There love is the meeting of two meteors in the middle of space, and not this obstinacy of rocks rubbing each other to ignite a sparking kiss.

Each night is an eyelid the thorns never stop piercing. And the day never ends, never stops counting itself, broken into copper coins. I am tired of so many stone beads scattered in the dust. I am tired of this unfinished solitaire. Lucky the mother scorpion who devours her young. Lucky the spider. Lucky the snake that sheds its skin. Lucky the water that drinks itself. When will these images stop devouring me? When will I stop falling in those empty eyes?

I am alone and fallen, grain of corn pulled from the ear of time. Sow me among the battle dead. I will be born in the captain's eye. Rain down on me, give me sun. My body, plowed by your body, will turn into a field where one is sown and a hundred reaped. Wait for me on the other side of the year: you will meet me like a lightning flash stretched to the edge of autumn. Touch my grass breasts. Kiss my belly, sacrificial stone. In my navel the whirlwind grows calm: I am the fixed center that moves the dance. Burn, fall into me: I am the pit of living lime that cures the bones of their afflictions. Die in my lips. Rise from my eyes. Images gush from my body: drink in these waters and remember what you forgot at birth. I am the wound that does not heal, the small solar stone: if you strike me, the world will go up in flames.

Take my necklace of tears. I wait for you on this side of time where light has inaugurated a joyous reign: the covenant of the enemy twins, water, that escapes between our fingers, and ice, petrified like a king in his pride. There you will open my body to read the inscription of your fate.

[E.W.]

# A poet

"Music and bread, milk and wine, love and sleep: free. Great mortal embrace of enemies that love each other: every wound is a fountain. Friends sharpen their weapons well, ready for the final dialogue to the end of time. The lovers cross the night enlaced, conjunction of stars and bodies. Man is the food of man. Knowledge is no different from dreaming, dreaming from doing. Poetry has set fire to all poems. Words are finished, images are finished. The distance between the name and the thing is abolished; to name is to create, and to imagine, to be born."

*"For now, grab your hoe, theorize, be punctual. Pay your price and collect your salary. In your free time, graze until you burst: there are huge meadows of newspapers. Or, blow up every night at the café table, your tongue swollen with politics. Shut up or make noise: it's all the same. Somewhere they've already sentenced you. There is no way out that does not lead to dishonor or the gallows: your dreams are too clear,* you need a strong philosophy."

[E.W.]

# Huastec lady

She walks by the riverbank, naked, healthy, newly bathed, newly born from the night. On her breast burn jewels wrenched from summer. Covering her sex, the withered grass, the blue, almost black grass that grows on the rim of the volcano. On her belly an eagle spreads its wings, two enemy flags entwine, and water rests. She comes from afar, from the humid country. Few have seen her. I will tell her secret: by day, she is a stone on the side of the road; by night, a river that flows to the flank of man.

[E.W.]

# Toward the poem

I

*Words, the profits of a quarter-hour wrenched from the charred tree of language, between the good mornings and the good nights, doors that enter and exit and enter on a corridor that goes from noplace to nowhere.*

*We turn and turn in the animal belly, in the mineral belly, in the belly of time. To find the way out: the poem.*

*Stubbornness of that face where my gazes are broken. Armed mind, unconquered before a countryside in ruins after the assault on the secret. Volcanic melancholy.*

*The benevolent papier-mâché pout of the Chief, the Leader, fetish of the century: the I, you, he, spinners of spider webs, pronouns armed with fingernails; faceless divinities, abstractions. He and we, We and He, nobody and no one. God the Father avenges himself in all these idols.*

*The moment freezes, compact whiteness that blinds and does not answer and dissolves, iceberg pushed by circular currents. It must return.*

*To rip off the masks of fantasy, to drive a spike into the sensitive center: to provoke the eruption.*

*To cut the umbilical cord, kill the Mother: the crime that the modern poet has committed for all, in the name of all. The young poet must discover Woman.*

*To speak for the sake of speaking, to wrench sounds from the desperate, to take dictation from the fly's flight, to blacken. Time splits in two: hour of the somersault.*

II

*Words, phrases, syllables, stars that turn around a fixed center. Two bodies, many beings that meet in a word. The paper is covered with indelible letters that no one spoke, that no one dictated, that have fallen there and ignite and burn and go out. This is how poetry exists, how love exists. And if I don't exist, you do.*

*Everywhere solitary prisoners begin to create the words of the new dialogue.*

*The spring of water. The mouthful of health. A girl reclining on her past. The wine, the fire, the guitar, the tablecloth. A red velvet wall in a village square. The cheers, the shining cavalry entering the city, the citizens in flight: hymns! Eruption of the white, the green, the flaming. Poetry: the easiest thing, that which writes itself.*

*The poem creates a loving order. I foresee a sun-man and a moon-woman, he free of his power, she of her slavery, and implacable loves streaking through black space. Everything must yield to those incandescent eagles.*

*Song dawns on the turrets of your mind. Poetic justice burns fields of shame: there is no room for nostalgia, for the I, for proper nouns.*

*Every poem is fulfilled at the poet's expense.*

*Future noon, huge tree of invisible leaves. In the plazas, men and women sing the solar song, fountain of transparencies. The yellow surf covers me: nothing mine will speak through my mouth.*

*When History sleeps, it speaks in dreams: on the forehead of the sleeping people, the poem is a constellation of blood. When History wakes, image becomes act, the poem happens: poetry moves into action.*

*Deserve your dream.*

[E.W.]

21

# Hymn among the ruins

*Where foams the Sicilian sea . . .*

Góngora

Self crowned the day displays its plumage.
A shout tall and yellow,
impartial and beneficent,
a hot geyser into the middle sky!
Appearances are beautiful in this their momentary truth.
The sea mounts the coast,
clings between the rocks, a dazzling spider;
the livid wound on the mountain glistens;
a handful of goats becomes a flock of stones;
the sun lays its gold egg upon the sea.
All is god.
A broken statue,
columns gnawed by the light,
ruins alive in a world of death in life!

*Night falls on Teotihuacán.*
*On top of the pyramid the boys are smoking marijuana,*
*harsh guitars sound.*
*What weed, what living waters will give life to us,*
*where shall we unearth the word,*
*the relations that govern hymn and speech,*
*the dance, the city and the measuring scales?*
*The song of Mexico explodes in a curse,*
*a colored star that is extinguished,*
*a stone that blocks our doors of contact.*
*Earth tastes of rotten earth.*

Eyes see, hands touch.
Here a few things suffice:
prickly pear, coral and thorny planet,
the hooded figs,
grapes that taste of the resurrection,
clams, stubborn maidenheads,
salt, cheese, wine, the sun's bread.

An island girl looks on me from the height of her duskiness,
a slim cathedral clothed in light.
A tower of salt, against the green pines of the shore,
the white sails of the boats arise.
Light builds temples on the sea.

*New York, London, Moscow.*
*Shadow covers the plain with its phantom ivy,*
*with its swaying and feverish vegetation,*
*its mousy fur, its rats swarm.*
*Now and then an anemic sun shivers.*
*Propping himself on mounts that yesterday were cities,*
    *Polyphemus yawns.*
*Below, among the pits, a herd of men dragging along.*
*(Domestic bipeds, their flesh—*
*despite recent religious prohibitions—*
*is much-loved by the wealthy classes.*
*Until lately people considered them unclean animals.)*

To see, to touch each day's lovely forms.
The light throbs, all darties and wings.
The wine-stain on the tablecloth smells of blood.
As the coral thrusts branches into the water
I stretch my senses to this living hour:
the moment fulfills itself in a yellow harmony.
Midday, ear of wheat heavy with minutes,
eternity's brimming cup.

*My thoughts are split, meander, grow entangled,*
*start again,*
*and finally lose headway, endless rivers,*
*delta of blood beneath an unwinking sun.*
*And must everything end in this spatter of stagnant water?*

Day, round day,
shining orange with four-and-twenty bars,
all one single yellow sweetness!
Mind embodies in forms,
the two hostile become one,
the conscience-mirror liquifies,

once more a fountain of legends:
man, tree of images,
words which are flowers become fruits which are deeds.

*Naples, 1948*                                   [W.C.W.]

# Is there no way out?

Dozing I hear an incessant
    river running between dimly discerned, looming
    forms, drowsy and frowning.
It is the black and white cataract, the voices,
    the laughter, the groans, of a confused
    world hurling itself from a height.
And my thoughts that gallop and gallop and get
    no further also fall and rise, and turn
    back and plunge into the stagnant waters of
    language.
A second ago it would have been easy to grasp a
    word and repeat it once and then again,
any one of those phrases one utters alone in a
    room without mirrors
to prove to oneself that it's not certain,
                     that we are still alive after all,
but now with weightless hands night is lulling the
    furious tide, and one by one images recede,
    one by one words cover their faces.

The time is past already for hoping for time's
    arrival, the time of yesterday, today and tomorrow,
yesterday is today, tomorrow is today, today all
    is today, suddenly it came forth from itself
    and is watching me,
it doesn't come from the past, it is not going
    anywhere, today is here, it is not death—
no one dies of death, everyone dies of life—it

is not life—instantaneous fruit, vertiginous
and lucid rapture, the empty taste of death
gives more life to life—
today is not death nor life,
has no body, nor name, nor face, today is here,
cast at my feet, looking at me.

I am standing, quiet at the center of the circle
I made in falling away from my thoughts,
I am standing and I have nowhere to turn my eyes
to, not one splintered fragment of the past
is left,
all childhood has brought itself to this instant
and the whole future is these pieces of
furniture nailed to their places,
the wardrobe with its wooden face, the chairs
lined up waiting for nobody,
the chubby armchair with its arms spread, obscene
as if dead in its bed,
the electric fan—conceited insect—the lying
window, the actual without chinks or cracks,
all has shut itself up in itself, I have come back
to where I began, everything is today and
forever.

Way off there, on the other side, shores extend,
immense as a look of love,
there the night clothed in water displays its
hieroglyphs within hand's reach,
the river enters singing along the sleeping plain
and moistens the roots of the word freedom,
there enlaced bodies lose themselves in a forest
of transparent trees,
under the leaves of the sun we walk, we
are two reflections that cross swords with
each other,
silver stretches bridges for us to cross the night,
stones make way for us,
there you are the tattooing on the jade breast fallen
from the moon, there the insomniac diamond
yields

and in its empty center we are the eye that never
   blinks and the transfixion of the instant
   held within itself in its splendor.

All is far off, there is no way back, the dead
   are not dead, the living are not alive,
there is a wall, an eye that is a well, all that is
   pulls downwards, the body is heavy,
thoughts are heavy, all the years are this minute
   that is dropping interminably down,
from that hotel room in San Francisco I stepped
   right into Bangkok, today is yesterday,
   tomorrow is yesterday,
reality is a staircase going neither up nor down,
   we don't move, today is today, always is today,
always the sound of trains that depart each night
   towards night,
the resort to toothless words,
the boring through of the wall, the comings and
   goings, reality shutting doors,
putting in commas, the punctuation of time, all
   is far off, the walls are enormous,
the glass of water is thousands of miles away, it
   will take me a thousand years to cross my
   room again,
what a remote sound the word life has, I am not
   here, there is no here, this room is some-
   where else, here is nowhere, little by little
   I have been shutting myself and I find no
   exit that doesn't give onto this instant,
this instant is I, I went out of myself all at
   once, I have no name and no face,
I am here, cast at my feet, looking at myself
   looking to see myself seen.

Outside, in the gardens that summer has ravaged
   a cicada rages against the night.
Am I or was I here?
                    *Tokyo, 1952*                    [D.L.]

26

# The river

The restless city circles in my blood like a bee.
And the plane that traces a querulous moan in a long S, the
   trams that break down on remote corners,
that tree weighted with affronts that someone shakes at midnight
   in the plaza,
the noises that rise and shatter and those that fade away and
   whisper a secret that wriggles in the ear,
they open the darkness, precipices of a's and o's, tunnels of
   taciturn vowels,
galleries I run down blindfolded, the drowsy alphabet falls in the
   pit like a river of ink,
and the city goes and comes and its stone body shatters as it
   arrives at my temple,
all night, one by one, statue by statue, fountain by fountain,
   stone by stone, the whole night long
its shards seek one another in my forehead, all night long the
   city talks in its sleep through my mouth,
a gasping discourse, a stammering of waters and arguing stone,
   its story.

To stop still an instant, to still my blood which goes and comes,
   goes and comes and says nothing,
seated on top of me like a yogi in the shadow of a fig tree, like
   Buddha on the river's edge, to stop the instant,
a single instant, seated on the edge of time, to strike out my
   image of the river that talks in its sleep and says nothing and
   carries me with it,
seated on the bank to stop the river, to unlock the instant, to
   penetrate its astonished rooms reaching the center of water,
to drink at the inexhaustible fountain, to be the cascade of blue
   syllables falling from stone lips,
seated on the edge of night like Buddha on his self's edge, to be
   the flicker of the lidded instant,
the conflagration and the destruction and the birth of the instant,
   the breathing of night rushing enormous at the edge of time,
to say what the river says, a long word resembling lips, a long
   word that never ends,

to say what time says in hard sentences of stone, in vast gestures
    of sea covering worlds.

In mid-poem a great helplessness overtakes me, everything
    abandons me,
there is no one beside me, not even those eyes that gaze from
    behind me at what I write,
no one behind or in front of me, the pen mutinies, there is
    neither beginning nor end nor even a wall to leap,
the poem is a deserted esplanade, what's said is not said, the
    unsaid is unsayable,
towers, devastated terraces, Babylons, a sea of black salt, a blind
    kingdom,
            No,
to stop myself, to keep quiet, to close my eyes until a green spike
    sprouts from my eyelids, a spurt of suns,
and the alphabet wavers long under the wind of the vision and
    the tide rolls into one wave and the wave breaks the dike,
to wait until the paper is covered with stars and the poem a
    forest of tangled words,
            No,
I have nothing to say, no one has anything to say, nothing and
    nobody except the blood,
nothing except this coming and going of the blood, this writing
    over the written, the repetition of the same word in mid-poem,
syllables of time, broken letters, splotches of ink, blood that goes
    and comes and says nothing and carries me with it.

And I speak, my beak bent over the paper and someone beside
    me writes while the blood goes and comes,
and the city goes and comes through his blood, wants to say
    something, time wants to say something, the night wants to
    speak,
all night long the man wants to say one single word, to speak his
    discourse at last, made up of moldered stones,
and I whet my hearing, I want to hear what the man says, to
    repeat what the drifting city says,
all night the broken stones seek one another, groping in my
    forehead, all night the water fights the stone,
the words against the night, the night against the night, nothing
    lights up the opaque combat,

the shock of arms does not wrench away a single gleam to the
   stone, one spark to the night, no one grants a respite,
it is a fight to the death between immortals,
                                        No,
to offer retreat, to stop the river of blood, the river of ink,
to go back upstream, and that the night turn upon itself
   display its bowels,
and that the water show its heart, a cluster of drowned mirrors,
may time thicken and its wound be an invisible scar, scarcely
   a delicate line upon the skin of the world,
let the words lay down their arms and the poem be one single
   interwoven word,
and may the soul be the blackened grass after fire, the lunar
   breast of a sea that's turned to stone and reflects nothing
except splayed dimension, expansion, space lying down upon
   itself, spread wings immense,
and may everything be like flame that cuts itself into and freezes
   into the rock of diaphanous bowels,
hard blazing resolved now in crystal, peaceable clarity.

And the river goes back upstream, strikes its sails, picks up its
   images and coils within itself.

*Geneva, 1953*                              [P.B.]


# Sun stone

> *La treizième revient . . . c'est encor la première;*
> *et c'est toujours la seule—ou c'est le seul moment;*
> *car es-tu reine, ô toi, la première ou dernière?*
> *es-tu roi, toi le seul ou le dernier amant?*
>                     Gérard de Nerval, "Arthémis"


willow of crystal, a poplar of water,
a pillar of fountain by the wind drawn over,
tree that is firmly rooted and that dances,
turning course of a river that goes curving,

advances and retreats, goes roundabout,
arriving forever:
                    the calm course of a star
or the spring, appearing without urgency,
water behind a stillness of closed eyelids
flowing all night and pouring out prophecies,
a single presence in the procession of waves,
wave over wave until all is overlapped,
in a green sovereignty without decline
a bright hallucination of many wings
when they all open at the height of the sky,

course of a journey among the densities
of the days of the future and the fateful
brilliance of misery shining like a bird
that petrifies the forest with its singing
and the annunciations of happiness
among the branches which go disappearing,
hours of light even now pecked away by the birds,
omens which even now fly out of my hand,

an actual presence like a burst of singing,
like the song of the wind in a burning building,
a long look holding the whole world suspended,
the world with all its seas and all its mountains,
body of light as it is filtered through agate,
the thighs of light, the belly of light, the bays,
the solar rock and the cloud-colored body,
color of day that goes racing and leaping,
the hour glitters and assumes its body,
now the world stands, visible through your body,
and is transparent through your transparency,

I go a journey in galleries of sound,
I flow among the resonant presences
going, a blind man passing transparencies,
one mirror cancels me, I rise from another,
forest whose trees are the pillars of magic,
under the arches of light I go among
the corridors of a dissolving autumn,

I go among your body as among the world,
your belly the sunlit center of the city,
your breasts two churches where are celebrated
the great parallel mysteries of the blood,
the looks of my eyes cover you like ivy,
you are a city by the sea assaulted,
you are a rampart by the light divided
into two halves, distinct, color of peaches,
and you are saltiness, you are rocks and birds
beneath the edict of concentrated noon,

and dressed in the coloring of my desires
you go as naked as my thoughts go naked,
I go among your eyes as I swim water,
the tigers come to these eyes to drink their dreams,
the hummingbird is burning among these flames,
I go upon your forehead as on the moon,
like cloud I go among your imagining
journey your belly as I journey your dream,

your loins are harvest, a field of waves and singing,
your loins are crystal and your loins are water,
your lips, your hair, the looks you give me, they
all night shower down like rain, and all day long
you open up my breast with your fingers of water,
you close my eyelids with your mouth of water,
raining upon my bones, and in my breast
the roots of water drive deep a liquid tree,

I travel through your waist as through a river,
I voyage your body as through a grove going,
as by a footpath going up a mountain
and suddenly coming upon a steep ravine
I go the straitened way of your keen thoughts
break through to daylight upon your white forehead
and there my spirit flings itself down, is shattered
now I collect my fragments one by one
and go on, bodiless, searching, in the dark,

the limitless corridors of memory
the doors that open on empty living-rooms
where every springtime withers and rots away
the jewels of thirst are burning at the base,
the face obliterated at memory,
the hand which will dissolve if I even touch it,
threads of those spider-webs in chaos over
the smiling of a past that falls away,

I search where I come face to face with daylight,
search without finding, I search for a moment,
for a face of lightning-flash and thunderstorm
running among the enormous trees of night,
face of all rain in a garden of shadows,
insistent water that flows along my side,

I search without finding, and I write alone,
no one is here, and the day ends, the year ends,
I have gone down with the moment, all the way down,
the road is invisible over all these mirrors,
they repeat and reflect forever my broken image,
I pace the days, the moments pave this roadway,
I step upon the thinking of my shadow,
I pace my shadow in search of my one moment,

I seek the day live as a live bird,
I seek the five o'clock sun of afternoon
tempered red by the red walls of *tezontle*:
an afternoon hour, ripening its clusters,
and as it bursts the girls emerge in light
from that rose-colored center and they scatter
out from the terrace of the college building,
tall as the autumn one girl walking onward
involved in light among the far arcades
and space girdles her round in a bright garment
of a new body more golden and transparent,

a tiger the color of light, a dark-brown deer
loping along the outskirts of the night,
a girl glimpsed once as she that once reclined

32

along the greenest balconies of the rain,
the endless unnumbered adolescent face,
I have forgotten your name, was it Melusine,
Laura, Isabel, Mary, Persephone,
your face is all their faces and none of them,
you are all the times and never any of them,
you take on the likeness of a tree, a cloud,
you are all birds and now you are a star,
now you resemble the sharp edge of a sword
and now the executioner's bowl of blood,
the encroaching ivy that overgrows and then
roots out the soul and divides it from itself,

writing of fire on the slab of jade,
the cleft in the rock, serpent-goddess and queen,
pillar of cloud, and fountain struck from the stone,
the nest of eagles, the circle of the moon,
the seed of anise, mortal and smallest thorn
that has the power to give immortal pain,
shepherd of valleys underneath the sea
and guardian of the valley of the dead,
liana that hangs at the pitch of vertigo,
climber and bindweed and the venomous plant,
flower of resurrection and grape of life,
lady of the flute and of the lightning-flash,
terrace of jasmine, and salt rubbed in the wound,
a branch of roses for the man shot down,
snowstorm in August, moon of the harrowing,
the writing of the sea cut in basalt,
the writing of the wind upon the desert,
testament of the sun, pomegranate, wheat-ear,

a face of flames, face that is eaten away,
the adolescent and persecuted face
the years of fantasy and circular days
that open upon the same street, the same wall,
the moment flares up and they are all one face,
the procession of faces of this calling,
all of these names are unified in one name,
all of these faces are now a single face,

all centuries are now a single instant
and throughout the centuries of centuries
the path to the future shut by these two eyes,

there is nothing before me, but a moment
recovered tonight, standing against a dream
that is dreamed of images all intertwined,
sculptured in permanence against the dream:
a moment torn from the zero of this night,
lifted up forcibly, feature by feature,
meanwhile, beyond it, time, spilling its guts,
and hammering, banging on the door of my soul,
the world, with its blood-spattered calendar,

only a moment while the capitals,
the names, strong flavors, the brightness of all things
crumble away within my sightless forehead,
while the mute heavy grieving of the night
beats down my thinking and my skeleton
and my blood courses more deliberately
and now my teeth begin to relent, my eyes
begin to cloud over; and the days and years
go heaping up their high and empty horrors,

time in an ancient gesture folds its fan
and there is nothing behind its images
the moment plunges into itself and floats
encircled by death among the threatenings
of the enormous mournful yawn of midnight,
and wholly threatened by the hullabaloo
of death enlivened by energy and masked,
the moment plunges and it pierces itself,
closes as a fist closes, like a perfect
fruit that ripens inwards in its own good time
spontaneously, drinks itself, and scatters,
the numinous moment shines, pierces itself,
and ripens inward, ripens and puts forth roots,
it grows within me, it completely fills me,
lavishes out on me delirious branches,
the thoughts flying within me are its birds,

and in my veins its mercury circulates,
the tree of the mind, its fruit tasting of time,

and life! to be lived, vivid nevertheless,
time that turns into a great surf approaching,
withdrawing without ever turning back,
the past is not the past, but it is here, now,
and in the silence of the present, it fills
into another moment which vanishes:

facing an afternoon, stone and saltpeter,
an enormous fleet of invisible razors,
you write a red and indecipherable
writing upon my skin and these open wounds
cover my body, a burning suit of flame,
I burn and am not consumed, I long for water,
and in your eyes there is no water, but stone,
your breasts are stone, your belly is stone, your loins
are made of stone, your mouth has the taste of dust,
your mouth tastes to me of an envenomed time,
your body has the taste of a pit without
any exit, a hall of mirrors reflecting
the eyes of one thirsty man, a corridor
returning forever to its starting point,
and I in blindness, you take me by the hand
along these endless obstinate galleries
into the center of this circle; erect,
you stand like lightning frozen into an axe,
the flaying light drawing and fascinating
as the built scaffold of death to the condemned,
flexible as a braided whip and slender
a twin weapon, a weapon like the moon,
and keenness of your speaking penetrates
my breast, leaving me empty and desolate,
you rip up all my memories by the roots,
I have forgotten my name, and now my friends
go grunting among the hogs, or lie and rot
eaten by the sun, beneath the precipice,

now there is nothing in me but one vast wound,
a gap with no possible way of healing,
a now without windows, a turn of intellect
moving on itself, repeating and reflecting,
it loses itself in its own transparency,
self-knowledge that is shot through by the eye
that watches itself watching, drowning itself
in clarity:
                    I saw your frightful armor,
Melusine, at dawn, in your green scales burning,
you slept, in coils and entangled with the sheets,
and like a bird you shrieked on awakening
whitened and dwindled away, endlessly, broken,
nothing remained of you except that shrieking,
and at the end of the years, I find myself
with a cough and poor eyesight, turning over
old photographs:
                         nobody, you were no one,
nobody, a heap of ashes and a broom,
a knife with a notched edge, a feather duster,
a few feet of skin suspended on some bones,
a dried-out bunch of something, a black hole
and there at the bottom of the hole two eyes
eyes of a girl drowned a thousand years ago,

those looks buried at the bottom of the pit,
looking at us from the beginning of time,
the young girl in her seeing an old mother
who sees within her grown son a young father,
the mother's seeing of a lonely daughter
who sees in the kingly father a young son,
looks that look into us to the furthest depth
of life, that are the traps and snares of death
—is it the opposite? is falling in those eyes
the way back to the true and central life?

to fall, to return, to dream, and let me be
the dream of the eyes of the future, another life,
other clouds, and die at last another death!
—tonight is my life, and this single moment

which never stops opening, never stops revealing
where my life lay, who I was, what your name is
and what my own name is:
                              was it I planning
for summer coming—and all coming summers—
in Christopher Street—this was ten years ago—
with Phyllis in the bright hollows of whose throat
the sparrows could come to drink, drinking the light?
on the Reforma did Carmen say to me
'this air is dry, it's always October here',
or did the other one say that, the one I lost,
or did I invent it, did nobody say it to me?
Was it I riding through a Oaxaca night
that was black-green and enormous, like a tree,
soliloquizing like the fantastic wind;
coming back to my room—always a room somewhere—
could the mirrors really not recognize me?
at the Hotel Vernet did we see dawn
dance with the chestnut trees—'it's late already'—
and did you do your hair and did I watch
the stains on the wall without saying a word?
did we go up the tower together, and see
the day descending on the outer reef?
did we eat grapes at Bidart? was it we
buying gardenias at Perote?
                              names, places,
streets and streets, faces, streets, circles,
railway stations, a park, the single rooms,
stains on the wall, somebody combing her hair,
somebody singing beside me, somebody dressing,
rooms, places, streets, names, rooms,

Madrid, nineteen hundred and thirty-seven,
on the Plaza del Angel seeing the women
doing their sewing and singing with their sons,
and then the shriek of the siren and their shriek,
houses brought down and crawling in the dust,
the towers cloven, the faces running spittle
and the hurricane of engines, I hold static:
two naked people loving one another

for the sake of defending our eternal portion,
our rationing of time and of paradise,
to touch our root, to reach ourselves in touching,
to recover our inheritance pirated
by robbers of life in a thousand centuries,
these two took their clothes off and they kissed
because these nakednesses, woven together,
can overleap time and are invulnerable,
nothing can touch them, they go to the origins,
there is no You nor I, tomorrow, yesterday, names,
there truly two become only one body and soul,
O total being . . .

                  there are rooms that are adrift
among the great cities that go foundering,
furnished rooms, city streets, names striking like wounds,
the room whose windows look out on other rooms
all papered in the same discoloured paper
where a man in shirt-sleeves reads his newspaper
or a woman irons; the room lit bright in spring
and, entering, the branches of the peach tree;
the other room: outside it is always raining,
there is a courtyard with three rusted children,
rooms that are ships, and that are rocking and singing
in a gulf of brilliance; or the submarines:
silence dispersed upon the greenness of waves
and everything that we touch phosphoresces;
memorials to a luxury whose pictures
are eaten away over the threadbare carpets;
trap-doors, cells, oubliettes, enchanted caverns,
cages of birds, and rooms with numbers on them,
everything is transfigured, everything is in flight,
all these moldings are clouds, and every door
opens on the sea, the field, the air; each meal
is now a celebration; sealed tight as shells,
time cannot hope, besieging them, to conquer,
there is no time here, no wall: space, space is here,
open your hand and gather these riches in,
cut all the fruits, this life is here to eat,
lie at the foot of this tree, and drink the water!

everything is transfigured and is sacred,
and each room is now the center of the world,
tonight is the first night, today the first day,
whenever two people kiss the world is born,
a drop of light with guts of transparency
the room like a fruit splits and begins to open
or burst like a star among the silences
and all laws now rat-gnawed and eaten away,
barred windows of banks and penitentiaries,
the bars of paper, and the barbed-wire fences,
the stamps and the seals, the sharp prongs and the spurs,
the one-note sermon of the bombs and wars,
the gentle scorpion in his cap and gown,
the tiger who is the president of the Society
for the Prevention of Cruelty and the Red Cross,
the pedagogical ass, and the crocodile
set up as savior, father of his country,
the founder, the leader, the shark, the architect
of the future of us all, the hog in uniform,
and then that one, the favorite son of the Church
who can be seen brushing his black teeth
in holy water and taking evening courses
in English and democracy, the invisible
barriers, the mad and decaying masks
that are used to separate us, man from man,
and man from his own self
                                    they are thrown down
for an enormous instant and we see darkly
our own lost unity, how vulnerable it is
to be women and men, the glory it is to be man
and share our bread and share our sun and our death,
the dark forgotten marvel of being alive;

to love is to struggle, and if two people kiss
the world is transformed, and all desires made flesh
and intellect is made flesh; great wings put forth
their shoots from the shoulders of the slave, the world
is real and to be touched and the wine is wine,
the bread can taste again, the water is water,
to love is to struggle, is to open the doors,

to stop being a fantasy with a number
condemned to the sentence of the endless chain
by a faceless master;
                        and the world is changed
when two people look at each other, recognizing
to love is to take off our clothes and our names:
'Allow me to be your whore', these are the words
of Heloise, but he gave in to the law,
he took her to be his wife, and as reward,
later, they castrated him;
                              better to have the crime,
the suicidal lovers, or the incest
between two brothers, as between two mirrors
falling in love and loving their reflections,
better to venture and eat the poisoned bread,
better adultery on beds of ashes,
the ferocious passions, and delirium,
its venomous ivy, and the sodomite
who carries for his buttonhole carnation
a gobbet of spit, better be killed by stoning
in the public square than tread the mill that grinds
out into nothing the substance of our life,
changes eternity into hollow hours,
minutes into penitentiaries, and time
into some copper pennies and abstract shit;

better take chastity, the invisible flower
swaying among the evening stalks of silence,
the difficult diamond of the saints of heaven
which filters out the desires and satiates time,
makes marriages of quietude and movement,
sings the song of solitude, her corolla,
a petal of crystal is, she sings, each hour,
the world is stripping itself of all its masks
and at its center, vibrating, transparent,
that being we call God, the nameless being,
contemplative of itself in nothingness,
the faceless being emerging from its self,
sun of suns, fullness of presences and names;
I follow my delirium, rooms, rooms, streets,

walk groping and groping down the corridors
of time and over and under its staircases
I feel along its walls and, not advancing,
I turn to where I began, I seek your face,
walk doubtfully these dim streets of my own self
under a timeless sun and you beside me
walk with me like a tree, a river going
walk with me speaking to me like a river,
grow like a stalk of wheat among my fingers,
throb like a squirrel warm among my fingers,
flying become a thousand birds, your smiling
has covered my body with sea-foam, your head
is a nebula in small between my hands,
the world grows fresh and green while you are smiling
and eating an orange
                              and the world is changed
if two people shaken by dizziness and enlaced
are fallen among the grass: the sky descending,
the trees pointing and climbing upward, and space
alone among all things is light and silence,
and pure space opens to the eagle of the eye,
and it sees pass the white tribe of the clouds,
the body's cables snap, the soul sails out,
now is the moment we lose our names, and float
along the border-line between blue and green,
the integrated time when nothing happens
but the event, belonging, communicating,

nothing happens, nothing, you become calm, blinking
(silence: an angel crosses over in this moment
enormous as the life of a hundred suns),
has nothing happened but the flickering eyelid?
—and the banquet, the exile, the first murder,
the jawbone of an ass, the city-battering sound
and the unbelieving gaze of the dead man
falling on the embers of the burning field,
and Agamemnon's lowing, immense howl,
the repetitious crying of Cassandra
a louder sound than the sound of waves crying,
and Socrates in chains (the sun is rising,

to die is to awake: 'Crito, I owe a
cock to Aesculapius, for being cured of life'),
the jackal who gives tongue among the ruins
of Nineveh, the shadow Brutus beheld
the night before the battle, Moctezuma
lying on his bed of thorns, insomnia,
the journey in the tumbril, the way to death
—the interminable journey made still longer
for Robespierre progressing inch by inch
holding his shattered jawbone in his hands—
Churruca acting as if his vat were a throne
of scarlet, and the measured steps of Lincoln
getting ready, that night, to go to theater,
the rattle in Trotsky's throat and then his moan
as of a wild boar, Madero and his gaze
answered by nobody: why are they killing me?
the balls, the guts, the alases, silences
of the saint, the criminal, and the poor devil,
graveyards of phrases and of those anecdotes
that the old dogs of rhetoric scratch over,
delirium, whinnying, the obscure noises
which have to do with death, this panting frenzy
of life getting itself born, the scraping sounds
of bones macerated in ferocity
and the mouth of foam that is the prophet's mouth
and his cry and the cry of the torturer
and the cry of the victim . . .
                              they are flames
the eyes are flames and those who gaze are flaming
the ear is fire and the fiery music,
live coal the lips and the tongue firebrand,
the one who touches and the one who is touching,
thinking and thought, and the thinker is a fire
and all things burn and the universe is flame,
and nothing burns like the rest, nothing which is
nothing except a thought in flames, ultimate smoke:
there is no victim and no torturer . . .
                              and the cry
that Friday afternoon? and then the silence
covering all the air with symbols, silence

which speaks without speaking, does it say nothing?
are they nothing at all, the cries of men?
does nothing happen in time but time passing?

—nothing happens, only the flickering eyelid
of the great sun, hardly a movement, nothing,
the unredeemable boundaries of time,
the dead are all pinned down by their own dying,
they cannot die again of another death,
they are untouchable, locked in their gestures,
and since their solitude and since their dying
this only can they do: stare sightless at us,
their death is simply the statue of their life,
perpetual being and nothingness without end,
for every moment is nothing without end,
a king of fantasy regulates your pulse
and your last gesture carves an impassive mask
and lays that sculpture over your mobile face:
we are the monument raised to an alien
life, a life unlived, not lively, hardly ours.

—and this our life, when was it truly ours?
and when are we truly whatever we are?
for surely we are not, we never are
anything alone but spinning and emptiness,
crazy faces made in the mirror, horror,
vomit; life is not ours, it is the others',
it is not anybody's, all of us are
life—the bread of the sun for all the others,
all of those others who are us, we ourselves—
I am the other when I am myself, my acts
are more my own when they are everybody's,
because to be myself I must be other,
go out of myself, seek my self among others,
those others who are not if I do not exist,
others give me the fullness of my existence,
I am not, there is no I, We are forever,
and life is otherwise, always *there*, farther,
beyond thee, beyond me, eternal horizon,
life that is dying for us, life that is made for

and invents us, our faces, eats them away,
the thirst for existence, death, bread of us all.

Heloise, Persephone, and Mary, thou,
turn to me then at last that you may see
my turn and central face, that of the other,
my face of us all, that is always all of us,
face of the living tree and the breadman,
the driver and the thunderhead, the sailor,
the sun's face, the arroyo's, faces of Peter and Paul,
face of the individual collective,
awaken me, now I am born:
                              life and death
are reconciled in thee, lady of midnight,
tower of clarity, empress of daybreak,
moon virgin, mother of all mother liquids,
body and flesh of the world, the house of death,
I have been endlessly falling since my birth,
I fall in my own self, never touch my depth,
gather me in your eyes, at last bring together
my scattered dust, make peace among my ashes,
bind the dismemberment of my bones, and breathe
upon my being, bring me to earth in your earth,
your silence of peace to the intellectual act
against itself aroused;
                              open now your hand
lady of the seeds of life, seeds that are days,
day is an immortality, it rises, it grows,
is done with being born and never is done,
every day is a birth, and every daybreak
another birthplace and I am the break of day,
we all dawn on the day, the sun dawns
and daybreak is the face of the sun, John
is the break of day with John's face, face of all,

gate of our being, awaken me, bring dawn,
grant that I see the face of the living day,
grant that I see the face of this live night,
everything speaks now, everything is transformed,
O arch of blood, bridge of our pulse beating,

carry me through to the far side of this night,
the place where I am You, equals Ourselves,
kingdom of persons and pronouns intertwined,

gateway of being: open your being, awaken,
learn then to be, begin to carve your face,
develop your elements, and keep your vision
keen to look at my face, as I at yours,
keen to look full at life right through to death,
faces of sea, of bread, of rock, of fountain,
the spring of origin which will dissolve our faces
in the nameless face, existence without face
the inexpressible presence of presences . . .

I want to go on, to go beyond; I cannot;
the moment scatters itself in many things,
I have slept the dreams of the stone that never dreams
and deep among the dreams of years like stones
have heard the singing of my imprisoned blood,
with a premonition of light the sea sang,
and one by one the barriers give way,
all of the gates have fallen to decay,
the sun has forced an entrance through my forehead,
has opened my eyelids at last that were kept closed,
unfastened my being of its swaddling clothes,
has rooted me out of my self, and separated
me from my animal sleep centuries of stone
and the magic of reflections resurrects
willow of crystal, a poplar of water,
a pillar of fountain by the wind drawn over,
tree that is firmly rooted and that dances,
turning course of a river that goes curving,
advances and retreats, goes roundabout,
arriving forever:

*Mexico City, 1957*                    [M.R.]

45

# Dawn

Cold rapid hands
draw back one by one
the bandages of dark
I open my eyes
                still
I am living
           at the center
of a wound still fresh

[C.T.]


# Here

My steps along this street
resound
         in another street
in which
         I hear my steps
passing along this street
in which

Only the mist is real

[C.T.]


# Landscape

Rock and precipice,
more time than stone, this
timeless matter.

46

Through its cicatrices
falls without moving
perpetual virgin water.

Immensity reposes here
rock on rock,
rocks over air.

The world's manifest
as it is: a sun
immobile, in the abyss.

Scale of vertigo:
the crags weigh
no more than our shadows.

[C.T.]


# Certainty


If it is real the white
light from this lamp, real
the writing hand, are they
real, the eyes looking at what I write?

From one word to the other
what I say vanishes.
I know that I am alive
between two parentheses.

[C.T.]

# Touch

My hands
open the curtains of your being
clothe you in a further nudity
uncover the bodies of your body
My hands
invent another body for your body

[C.T.]


# Duration

*"Thunder and wind: duration."*
I Ching

I

Sky black
       Yellow earth
The rooster tears the night apart
The water wakes and asks what time it is
The wind wakes and asks for you
A white horse goes by


II

As the forest in its bed of leaves
you sleep in your bed of rain
you sing in your bed of wind
you kiss in your bed of sparks


III

Multiple vehement odor
many-handed body

48

On an invisible stem a single
whiteness


IV

Speak listen answer me
what the thunder-clap
says, the woods
understand


V

I enter by your eyes
you come forth by my mouth
You sleep in my blood
I waken in your head


VI

I will speak to you in stone-language
(answer with a green syllable)
I will speak to you in snow-language
(answer with a fan of bees)
I will speak to you in water-language
(answer with a canoe of lightning)
I will speak to you in blood-language
(answer with a tower of birds)

[D.L.]


# Last dawn


Your hair lost in the forest,
your feet touching mine.
Asleep you are bigger than the night,
but your dream fits within this room.

49

How much we are who are so little!
Outside a taxi passes
with its load of ghosts.
The river that runs by
                    is always
running back.

Will tomorrow be another day?

[E.W.]

# Salamander

Salamander
            (the fire wears
            black armor)
a slow-burning stove
                    between the jaws
                    —marble or brick—
                    of the chimney it is
                    an ecstatic tortoise, a crouched
                    Japanese warrior:
whatever it is, martyrdom
is repose
impassive under torture

Salamander
ancient name of fire
                    and ancient
                    antidote to fire
flayed sole of the foot
on hot coals
amianthus *amante* amianthus

Salamander
in the abstract city between
dizzy geometries

50

—glass cement stone iron—
formidable chimeras appear
raised up by calculus
multiplied by profit
by the side of the anonymous wall
sudden poppy

Salamander
Yellow claw a scrawl
of red letters on a
wall of salt
        Claw of sunlight
        on a heap of bones

Salamander
fallen star
in the endlessness of bloodstained opal
ensepulchred
beneath eyelids of quartz
lost girl
in tunnels of onyx
in the circles of basalt
buried seed
        grain of energy
        in the marrow of granite

Salamander, you who lay dynamite in iron's
black and blue breast
you explode like a sun
you open yourself like a wound
you speak
        as a fountain speaks

Salamander
        blade of wheat
daughter of fire
spirit of fire
condensation of blood
sublimation of blood
evaporation of blood

Salamander of air
the rock is flame
              the flame is smoke
red vapor
              straight-rising prayer
lofty word of praise
exclamation
              crown
of fire on the head of the psalm
scarlet queen
(and girl with purple stockings
running disheveled through the woods)

Salamander, you are
silent, the
black consoler of sulfur tears
                    (One wet summer I heard
                    the vibration of your
                    cylindrical tail
                    between loose tiles of a
                    dead-calm moonlit patio)

Caucasian salamander
                    in the rock's
                    cindery shoulder appears
                    and disappears
                    a brief black tongue
                    flecked with saffron

Black and brilliant creature
the moss
quivers
you devour
insects
diminutive herald of the rain-shower
familiar spirit of the lightning
(Internal fecundation
oviparious reproduction
the young live in the water
once adult they swim sluggishly)

Salamander
Hanging bridge between eras
                              bridge of cold blood
axis of movement
(The changes in the alpine species
the most slender of all
take place in the mother's womb
Of all the tiny eggs no more than two mature
and until they hatch
the embryos are nourished on a broth
composed of the doughy mass of their aborted brother-eggs)

The Spanish Salamander
black and red mountaineer

The sun nailed to the sky's center does not throb
does not breathe
life does not commence without blood
without the embers of sacrifice
the wheel of days does not revolve
Xólotl refuses to consume himself
he hid himself in the corn but they found him
he hid himself in the maguey but they found him
he fell into the water and became the fish axólotl
the Double-Being
                    'and then they killed him'
Movement began, the world was set in motion
the procession of dates and names
Xólotl the dog, guide to Hell
he who dug up the bones of the fathers
he who cooked the bones in a pot
he who lit the fire of the years
the maker of men
Xólotl the penitent
the burst eye that weeps for us
Xólotl
        larva of the butterfly
        double of the Star
        sea-shell
        other face of the Lord of Dawn
Xólotl the axólotl

## Salamander

solar arrow
lamp of the moon
column of noonday
name of woman
scales of night

        (The infinite weight of light
        a half-drachm on your eyelashes)

Salamander
back flame
sunflower

      you yourself the sun
      the moon
      turning for ever around you
pomegranate that bursts itself open each night
fixed star on the brow of the sky
and beat of the sea and the stilled light
open mind above the
                to-and-fro of the sea

The star-lizard, salamandria
saurian scarcely eight centimeters long
lives in crevices and is the color of dust

Salamander of earth and water
green stone in the mouth of the dead
stone of incarnation
stone of fire
sweat of the earth
salt flaming and scorching
salt of destruction and
mask of lime that consumes the face

Salamander of air and fire

             wasp's nest of suns
             red word of beginning

The salamander
a lizard
her tongue ends in a dart

her tail ends in a dart
She is unhissable      She is unsayable
she rests upon hot coals
queens it over firebrands
If she carves herself in the flame
she burns her monument
Fire is her passion, her *patience*

Salamander                    Salamater

                                        [D.L.]


# Happiness in Herat

*For Carlos Pellicer*


I came here
as I write these lines,
at random:
a blue-and-green mosque,
six truncated minarets,
two or three tombs,
memories of a poet-saint,
the names of Timur and his lineage.

I met the wind of the hundred days.
It spread sand over all the nights.
It scourged my brow, scorched my lids.
Daybreak:
            dispersion of birds
and that sound of water among stones
which is the peasant's footsteps.
(But the water tasted of dust.)
Murmurs in the plain,
appearances
                disappearances,
ocher whirlwinds
insubstantial as my thoughts.
Wheeling and wheeling

in the hotel room, on the hills:
this land a camels' graveyard
and in my brooding
always the same crumbling faces.
Is the wind, the lord of ruins,
my only master?
Erosions:
minus grows more and more.

At the saint's tomb
I nailed a nail
deep into the lifeless tree,
                              not,
like the others, against the evil eye:
against myself.
(I said something—
words the wind took away.)

One afternoon the heights convened.
The poplars walked around
                              while standing still.
Sun on the glazed tiles
                              sudden springtimes.
In the Ladies' Garden
I climbed to the turquoise cupola.
Minarets tattooed with characters:
that Cufic script became clear
beyond its meaning.
I did not have the vision without images,
I did not see forms whirl till they disappeared
in immobile clarity,
in the Sufi's being-without-substance.
I did not drink plenitude in vacuity
nor see the two and thirty signs
of the Bodhisattva's diamond-body.
I saw a blue sky and all the shades of blue,
and the white to green
of the spread fan of the poplars,
and, on the tip of the pine tree,
the black-and-white ouzel,

less bird than air.
I saw the world resting upon itself.
I saw the appearances.
And I named that half-hour:
Perfection of the Finite.

[L.K.]

# Apparition

If man is dust
those who go through the plain
are men

[C.T.]

# In the Lodi gardens

*For Claude Esteban*

The black, pensive, dense
domes of the mausoleums
suddenly shot birds
into the unanimous blue

[E.W.]

# The other

He invented a face for himself.
                              Behind it,
he lived, died, and was resurrected
many times.
              Today his face
has the wrinkles of that face.
His wrinkles have no face.

                                        [E.W.]


# Vrindaban

Surrounded by night
immense forest of breathing
vast impalpable curtains
murmurs
              I write
I stop
        I write

              (All is and is not
and it all falls apart on the page
in silence)

              A moment ago
a car raced down the street
among the extinguished houses
                              I raced
among my lighted thoughts
Above me the stars
                    such quiet gardens
I was a tree and spoke

58

was covered with leaves and eyes
was the rumor pushing forward
a swarm of images

(I set down now a few
twisted strokes
                black on white
diminutive garden of letters
planted in the lamp's light)

The car raced on
through the sleeping suburb
                        I raced
to follow my thoughts
                    mine and others
Reminiscences left-overs imaginings
names
        The remains of sparks
        the laughter of the late parties
        the dance of the hours
        the march of the constellations
and other commonplaces
Do I believe in man
                or in the stars?
I believe
        (with here a series
of dots)
        I see

A portico of weather-eaten pillars
statues carved by the plague
a double line of beggars
                        and the stench
a king on his throne
                    surrounded
by a coming and going of aromas
as if they were concubines
pure almost corporeal undulating
from the sandalwood to the jasmine
and its phantoms

Putrefaction
                fever of forms
                                fever of time
ecstatic in its combinations
The whole universe a peacock's tail
myriads of eyes
                        other eyes reflecting
modulations
                    reverberations of a single eye
a solitary sun
                hidden
behind its cloth of transparencies
its tide of marvels
Everything was flaming
                            stones women water
Everything sculptured
                        from color to form
from form to fire
                        Everything was vanishing
Music of wood and metal
in the cell of the god
                    womb of the temple
Music
like the wind and water embracing
and over the entwined sounds
the human voice
a moon in heat at midday
stela of the disembodied soul

(I write without knowing the outcome
of what I write
                I look between the lines
My image is the lamp
                        lit
in the middle of the night)


                        Mountebank
ape of the Absolute
                cowering
pothook

60

covered with pale ashes
a sadhu looked at me and laughed
watching me from the other shore
                              far off, far off
watching me like the animals like the saints
Naked    uncombed    smeared
a fixed ray a mineral glitter his eyes
I wanted to speak to him
he answered with a rumble of bowels
                              Gone    gone
Where?
          To what region of being
to what existence
                    in the open air of what worlds
in what time?


              (I write
each letter is a germ
                    The memory
imposes its tide
and repeats its own midday)


Gone    gone
              Saint    scoundrel    saint
in beatitudes of hunger or drugs
Perhaps he saw Krishna
                         sparkling blue tree
dark fountain splashing amid the drought
Perhaps in a cleft stone
he grasped the form of woman
                              its rent
the formless dizziness
                    For this or that
he lives on the ghat where they burn the dead

The lonely streets
the houses and their shadows
All was the same and all different
The car raced on
              I was quiet

among my runaway thoughts

(Gone   gone
Saint   clown   saint   beggar   king   damned
it is the same
              always the same
                          within the same
It is to be always within oneself
closed up in the same
                    Closed up on oneself
rotted idol)


          Gone      gone
he watched me from the other shore
                          he watches me
from his interminable noon
I am in the wandering hour
The car races on among the houses
I write by the light of a lamp
The absolutes the eternities
their outlying districts
                    are not my theme
I am hungry for life and for death also
I know what I know and I write it
The embodiment of time
                    the act
the movement in which the whole being
is sculptured and destroyed
Consciousness and hands to grasp the hour
I am a history
              a memory inventing itself
I am never alone
I speak with you always
                    you speak with me always
I move in the dark
              I plant signs

                                        [L.K.]

# Village

The stones are time
                    The wind
centuries of wind
                    The trees are time
the people are stone
                    The wind
turns upon itself and sinks
into the stone day

There is no water here for all the luster of its eyes

                                                    [C.T.]


# Daybreak

Hands and lips of wind
heart of water
                    eucalyptus
campground of the clouds
the life that is born every day
the death that is born every life

I rub my eyes:
the sky walks the land

                                                    [E.W.]


63

# Nightfall

What sustains it,
half-open, the clarity of nightfall,
the light let loose in the gardens?

All the branches,
conquered by the weight of birds,
lean toward the darkness.

Pure, self-absorbed moments
still gleam
on the fences.

Receiving night,
the groves become
hushed fountains.

A bird falls,
the grass grows dark,
edges blur, lime is black,
the world is less credible.

[E.W.]

# On reading John Cage

Read
    unread:
*Music without measurements,*
*sounds passing through circumstances.*
I hear them within me
                passing outside,
I see them outside me
                passing within me.

I am the circumstance.
Music:
       I hear within what I see outside,
       I see within what I hear outside.
(I can't hear myself hearing: Duchamp.)
                                        I am
an architecture of sounds
instantaneous
                on
a space that disintegrates itself.
                        (*Everything*
*we come across is to the point.*)
                        Music
invents silence,
                architecture
invents space.
                Factories of air.
Silence
       is the space of music:
an unextended
                space:
                        there is no silence
save in the mind.
                Silence is an idea,
                the idée fixe of music.
Music is not an idea:
                        it is movement,
sounds walking over silence.
(*Not one sound fears the silence*
                        *That extinguishes it.*)
Silence is music,
                music is not silence.
Nirvana is Samsara,
                Samsara is not Nirvana.
Knowing is not knowing:
                        recovering ignorance,
knowledge of knowing.
                        It is not the same thing to hear
the footsteps of this afternoon
between the trees and houses
                        as it is

to see this same afternoon now
between the same trees and houses
                              after having read
*Silence:*
        Nirvana is Samsara,
                        silence is music.
(*Let life obscure*
                *the difference between art and life.*)
Music is not silence:
                    it is not saying
what silence says,
                    it is saying
what it doesn't say.
                    Silence has no sense,
                    sense has no silence.
Without being heard
                    music slips between both.
(*Every something is an echo of nothing.*)
In the silence of my room
                        the murmur of my body:
unheard.
        One day I shall hear its thoughts.
                                    The afternoon
stands still:
            yet—it walks.
My body hears the body of my wife
                            (*a cable of sound*)
and responds to it:
                    this is called music.
Music is real,
            silence is an idea.
John Cage is Japanese
                    and is not an idea:
he is sun on snow.
        /
                    Sun and snow are not the same:
sun is snow and snow is snow
                            or
sun is not snow and snow is not snow
or
   John Cage is not American

*(U.S.A. is determined to keep the Free World free,*
*U.S.A. determined)*
                    or
John Cage is American
                         *(that the U.S.A. may become*
*just another part of the world.*
                         *No more, no less.)*
Snow is not sun,
                 music is not silence,
sun is snow,
              silence is music.
*(The situation must be Yes-and-No,*
                              *not either-or)*
Between silence and music,
                          art and life,
snow and sun
              there is a man.
This man is John Cage
                      *(committed*
*to the nothing in between).*
                         He says a word:
not snow not sun,
                  one word
which is not
              silence:
*A year from Monday* you will hear it.

The afternoon has become invisible.
                                   [M.F.W. and G.A.]

# Writing

I draw these letters
as the day draws its images
and blows over them
                and does not return
                                   [E.W.]

67

# Concord

*For Carlos Fuentes*

        Water above
        Grove below
     Wind on the roads

        Quiet well
Bucket's black     Spring water

Water coming down to the trees
     Sky rising to the lips

                [E.W.]

# Exclamation

Stillness
        not on the branch
in the air
        not in the air
in the moment
           hummingbird

                [E.W.]

# Wind from all compass points

The present is motionless
The mountains are of bone and of snow
they have been here since the beginning
The wind has just been born
                              ageless
as the light and the dust
                              A windmill of sounds
the bazaar spins its colors
                              bells    motors    radios
the stony trot of dark donkeys
songs and complaints entangled
among the beards of the merchants
the tall light chiselled with hammer-strokes
In the clearings of silence
                         boys' cries
      explode
Princes in tattered clothes
on the banks of the tortured river
pray          pee          meditate


                              The present is motionless
The floodgates of the year open
                         day flashes out
            agate
      The fallen bird
between rue Montalambert and rue de Bac
is a girl
      held back
at the edge of a precipice of looks
If water is fire
            flame
                  dazzled
in the center of the spherical hour
            a sorrel filly
A marching battalion of sparks
                         a real girl

among wraithlike houses and people
Presence a fountain of reality
I looked out through my own unrealities
I took her hand
                         together we crossed
the four quadrants the three times
floating tribes of reflections
and we returned to the day of beginning


The present is motionless
                              June 21st
today is the beginning of summer
                                   Two or three birds
invent a garden
                    You read and eat a peach
on the red couch
                    naked
like the wine in the glass pitcher
                                   A great flock of crows
Our brothers are dying in Santo Domingo
'If we had the munitions
                              You people would not be here'
                    We chew our nails down to the elbow
In the gardens of his summer fortress
Tipoo Sultan planted the Jacobin tree
then distributed glass shards among
the imprisoned English officers
and ordered them to cut their foreskins
and eat them
                    The century
has set fire to itself in our lands
Will the builders of cathedrals and pyramids
charred hands
                    raise their transparent houses
by its light?


                    The present is motionless
The sun has fallen asleep between your breasts
The red covering is black and heaves
Not planet and not jewel
                              fruit

70

you are named
                        date
                        Datia
castle of Leave-If-You-Can
                                scarlet stain
upon the obdurate stone
Corridors
                terraces
                        stairways
dismantled nuptial chambers
of the scorpion
                        Echoes repetitions
the intricate and erotic works of a watch
                                        beyond time
                                        You cross

taciturn patios under the pitiless afternoon
a cloak of needles on your untouched shoulders
If fire is water
                you are a diaphanous drop
the real girl
                transparency of the world

The present is motionless
                                The mountains
                quartered suns
petrified storm earth-yellow
                        The wind whips
                                it hurts to see
The sky is another deeper abyss
                                Gorge of the Salang Pass
black cloud over black rock
Fist of blood strikes
                        gates of stone
Only the water is human
in these precipitous solitudes
Only your eyes of human water
                        Down there
in the cleft
desire covers you with its two black wings
Your eyes flash open and close
                        phosphorescent animals

Down there
            the hot canyon
the wave that stretches and breaks
                        your legs apart
the plunging whiteness
the foam of our bodies abandoned


                        The present is motionless
The hermit watered the saint's tomb
his beard was whiter than the clouds
Facing the mulberry
            on the flank of the rushing stream
you repeat my name
            dispersion of syllables
A young man with green eyes presented you
with a pomegranate
            On the other bank of the Amu-Darya
smoke rose from Russian cottages
The sound of an Usbek flute
was another river invisible clearer
The boatman
            on the barge was strangling chickens
The countryside is an open hand
                        its lines
            marks of a broken alphabet
Cow skeletons on the prairie
Bactria
      a shattered statue
I scraped a few names out of the dust
By these fallen syllables
seeds of a charred pomegranate
I swear to be earth and wind
                        whirling
over your bones


            The present is motionless
Night comes down with its trees
night of electric insects and silken beasts
night of grasses which cover the dead
meeting of waters which come from far off

rustlings
            universes are strewn about
a world falls
                a seed flares up
each word beats
                I hear you throb in the shadow
a riddle shaped like an hour-glass
                                woman asleep
Space    living spaces
Anima mundi
                maternal substance
always torn from itself
always falling into your empty womb
                                Anima mundi
mother of the nomadic tribes
                        of suns and men
The spaces turn
                the present is motionless


At the top of the world
Shiva and Parvati caress
                        Each caress lasts a century
for the god and for the man
                        an identical time
an equivalent hurling headlong
                        Lahore
                                red river black boats
a barefoot girl
                between two tamarinds
and her timeless gaze
                        An identical throbbing
death and birth
A group of poplars
suspended between sky and earth
they are a quiver of light more than a trembling of leaves
                        Do they rise
                                or fall?


The present is motionless
                It rains on my childhood

73

it rains on the feverish garden
flint flowers    trees of smoke
In a fig-leaf you sail
                          on my brow
The rain does not wet you
you are flame of water
                          the diaphanous drop of fire
spilling upon my eyelids
I look out through my own unrealities
the same day is beginning
                              Space wheels
the world wrenches up its roots
Our bodies
            stretched out
                          weigh no more than dawn

[P.B.]


# Madrigal


More transparent
than this water dropping
through the vine's twined fingers
my thought stretches a bridge
from yourself to yourself
                          Look at you
truer than the body you inhabit
fixed at the center of my mind

You were born to live on an island

[E.W.]

# With eyes closed

With eyes closed
you light up within
you are blind stone

Night after night I carve you
with eyes closed
you are frank stone

We have become enormous
just knowing each other
with eyes closed

[E.W.]


# Transit

Lighter than air
                    than water
than lips
         light light

Your body is the footprint of your body

[L.K.]

# Maithuna

My eyes discover you
naked
      and cover you
with a warm rain
of glances

                   •

A cage of sounds
               open
to the morning
            whiter
than your thighs
           at night
your laughter
         and more your foliage
your blouse of the moon
              as you leap from bed

Sifted light
        the singing spiral
spools whiteness
           Chiasm
X
  planted in a chasm

              •

My day
       exploded
in your night
         Your shriek
leaps in pieces
         Night
spreads
      your body
washing under
        your bodies

knot
Your body once again

        •


Vertical hour
        drought
spins its flashing wheels
Garden of knives
        feast of deceit
Through these reverberations
           you enter
unscathed
        the river of my hands

        •


Quicker than fever
you swim in darkness
        your shadow clearer
between caresses
        your body blacker
You leap
        to the bank of the improbable
toboggans of how when because yes
Your laughter burns your clothes
           your laughter
soaks my forehead my eyes my reasons
Your body burns your shadow
You swing on a trapeze of fear
the terrors of your childhood
        watch me
from your cliffhanging eyes
        wide-open
making love
        at the cliff
Your body clearer
        Your shadow blacker
You laugh over your ashes

        •

Burgundy tongue of the flayed sun
tongue that licks your land of sleepless dunes
hair unpinned
                    tongue of whips
                                   spoken tongues
unfastened on your back
                         enlaced
on your breasts
                    writing that writes you
with spurred letters
                       denies you
with branded signs
                      dress that undresses you
writing that dresses you in riddles
writing in which I am buried
                              Hair unpinned
the great night swift over your body
jar of hot wine
               spilled
on the tablets of the law
howling nude and silent cloud
cluster of snakes
                  cluster of grapes
trampled
        by the cold soles of the moon
rain of hands leaves fingers wind
on your body
              on my body on your body
Hair unpinned
               foliage of the tree of bones
the tree of aerial roots that drink night from the sun
The tree of flesh                The tree of death

                         •


Last night
          in your bed
we were three:
the moon      you & me

                         •

I open
        the lips of your night
damp hollows
                    unborn
echoes:


        whiteness
a rush
    of unchained water


                    •


To sleep to sleep in you
or even better to wake
                        to open my eyes
at your center
                    black white black
white
        To be the unsleeping sun
your memory ignites
                    (and
the memory of me in your memory


                    •


And again the sap skywise
rises
    (salvia your name
is flame)
            Sapling
crackling
            (rain
of blazing snow)
                    My tongue
is there
        (Your rose
burns through the snow)
                            is
now
    (I seal your sex)
                        dawn
from danger drawn

                                        [E.W.]


                                        79

# The key of water

After Rishikesh
the Ganges is still green.
The glass horizon
breaks among the peaks.
We walk upon crystals.
Above and below
great gulfs of calm.
In the blue spaces
white rocks, black clouds.
You said:
> *Le pays est plein de sources.*
That night I dipped my hands in your breasts.

[E.B.]


# Sunday on the island of Elephanta

IMPRECATION

At the feet of the sublime sculptures,
disfigured by the Muslims and the Portuguese,
the crowds have left a picnic of garbage
for the crows and dogs.
I condemn them to be reborn a hundred times
on a dungheap,
                and as for the others,
for eons they must carve living flesh
in the hell for the mutilators of statues.

Shiva and Parvati:
                    we worship you
not as gods
            but as images
of the divinity of man.
You are what man makes and is not,
what man will be
when he has served the sentence of hard labor.
Shiva:
        your four arms are four rivers,
four jets of water.
                    Your whole being is a fountain
where the lovely Parvati bathes,
where she rocks like a graceful boat.
The sea beats beneath the sun:
it is the great lips of Shiva laughing;
the sea is ablaze:
it is the steps of Parvati on the waters.
Shiva and Parvati:
                    the woman who is my wife
and I
      ask you for nothing, nothing
that comes from the other world:
                                only
the light on the sea,
the barefoot light on the sleeping land and sea.

                                              [E.W.]

# Blanco

*Blanco*: white; blank; an unmarked space; emptiness; void; the white mark in the center of a target.

As it is not possible to reproduce here all of the characteristics of the original edition of the poem, it should be mentioned that *Blanco* was meant to be read as a succession of signs on a single page. As the reading progresses, the page unfolds vertically: a space which, as it opens out, allows the text to appear and, in a certain sense, creates it. It is something like the motionless voyage offered by a roll of Tantric pictures and emblems: as we unroll it, a ritual is spread out before our eyes, a sort of procession or pilgrimage to—where? Space flows, engenders a text, dissolves it—it passes as though it were time. This arrangement of temporal order is the form adopted by the course of the poem: its discourse corresponds to another which is spatial: the separate parts which comprise the poem are distributed like the sections, colors, symbols, and figures of a mandala. . . . The typography and format of the original edition of *Blanco* were meant to emphasize not so much the presence of the text but the space that sustains it: that which makes writing and reading possible, that in which all writing and reading end.

*Blanco* is a composition that offers the possibility of variant readings:
a) in its totality, as a single text;
b) the center column, excluding those to the left and right, is a poem whose theme is the passage of the word from silence to silence, passing through four stages; yellow, red, green, and blue;
c) the lefthand column is a poem divided into four moments corresponding to the four traditional elements;
d) the righthand column is another poem, in counterpoint to the left, and composed of four variations on sensation, perception, imagination and understanding;
e) each of the four parts formed by the two columns may be read, ignoring the division, as a single text—four independent poems;
f) the center column may be read as six separate poems; those of the left and right as eight.

> *By passion the world is bound,*
> *by passion too it is released.*
> The Hevajra Tantra

> *Avec ce seul objet dont le*
> *Néant s'honore.*
> Stéphane Mallarmé


a stirring
          a starting
a seedling
          still sleeping
a word at the tongue's tip
unheard         inaudible
        incomparable
fertile           arid
       ageless
she buried with open eyes
blameless       promiscuous
      the word
speechless       nameless


Climbing and descending
the mineshaft ladder:
deserted language.
A lamp beats
beneath penumbra skin.
               Survivor
amidst sullen confusions,
            it rises
on a copper stem,
         resolves
into a foliage of clarities:
           retreat
for fallen realities.
         Asleep
or extinct,
      high on its pole
(head on a pike)
        a sunflower
charred light
      above a vase

of shadow.
                    In the palm
of a fictitious hand,
                              a flower
not seen nor thought:
                              heard,
appears,
             a yellow
chalice of consonants and vowels,
all burning.


the shadow of the fire on the wall   *flame circle by lions*
your shadow and mine in the fire   *lioness in the circus of the flames*
                                     *soul amidst sensations*
the fire knots and unlaces you
Bread Grail Coal                     *fireworks fruit*
                    Girl              *the senses open*
you laugh—naked                      *in the magnetic night*
in the gardens of the flame
          The passion of compassionate coals


A pulse-beat, insisting,
a surge of wet syllables.
Without saying a word
my forehead grows dark:
a presentiment of language.
*Patience patience*
(Livingston in the drought)
*River rising a little.*
Mine is red and is scorched
between flaming dunes:
Spanish castles of sand, shredded playing cards,
and the hieroglyph (coal and water)
fallen on the chest of Mexico.
I am the dust of that silt.
River of blood,
                    river of histories

of blood,
               dry river:
mouth of the source
                    gagged
by an anonymous conspiracy
of bones,
by the grim rock of centuries
and minutes:
                    language
is atonement,
                    an appeasement
of him who does not speak,
                              entombed,
assassinated
               every day,
the countless dead ones.
                              To speak
while others work
is to polish bones,
                    to sharpen
silences
          to transparency,
to undulation,
               the whitecap
to water:


the rivers of your body          *the river of bodies*
country of pulse-beats           *stars reptiles microorganisms*
to enter you                     *torrent of sleepwalking cinnabar*
country of closed eyes           *surge of genealogies*
water without thoughts           *games conjugations mimicries*
to enter me                      *subject and object abject and absolved*
entering your body               *river of suns*
country of sleepless mirrors     *"the tall beasts with shining skin"*
country of waking water          *seminal river of the worlds wheeling*
in the sleeping night            *the eye that watches it is another river*

watching I watch myself          *what I see is my creation*
as if to enter through my eyes   *perception is conception*

into an eye more crystal clear *water of thoughts*
what I watch watches me *I am the creation of what I watch*

delta of the arms of desire *water of truth*
on a bed of vertigo *truth of water*
          Transparency is all that remains


Desert burning
from yellow to flesh color:
the land is a charred language.
There are invisible spines, there are
thorns in the eyes.
          Three satiated vultures
on a pink wall.
It has no body no face no soul,
it is everywhere,
crushing all of us:
          this sun is unjust.
Rage is mineral.
          Colors
are relentless.
          Unrelenting horizon.
Drumbeats drumbeats drumbeats.
The sky blackens
          like this page.
Scattering of crows.
Impending violet violences.
The sand whirls up,
thunderheads, herds of ash.
The chained trees howl.
Drumbeats drumbeats drumbeats.
I pound you sky,
          land I pound you.
Open sky, closed land,
flute and drum, lightning and thunder,
I open you, I pound you.
          You open, land,
your mouth filled with water,
your body gushes sky,

you crack, land,
                    and burst,
          your seeds explode,
                              the word grows green.


unlaces spreads *arid undulation*
rises erects into an Idol *between arms of sand*
naked as the mind *shines multiplies self-denies*
in the reverberation of desire *is reborn escapes in self-pursuit*
turning turning *vision of hawk-thought*
around a black idea *goat in the rock cleft*
fleece at the joining *naked place*
in a naked woman *snapshot of a pulse-beat of time*
firefly tangle of beings *real unreal quiet vibrating*
unmoving beneath the sun unmoving *burnt meadow*
the color of earth *color of sun on sand*
the grass of my shadow *on the joining place*
my hands of rain *darkened by birds*
on your green breasts *holiness enough*
woman stretched out *made in the image of the world*
          The world a bundle of your images


From yellow to red to green,
a pilgrimage to the clarities,
the word peering out from blue
whirlpools.
          The drunk ring spins,
the five senses spin
around the centripetal
amethyst.
          Dazzlement:
I don't think, I see
                    —not what I see,
but the reflections, the thoughts I see.
The precipitations of music,
crystallized number.
An archipelago of signs.

Lucidity,
        mouth of truths,
clarity effaced in a syllable
translucid as silence:
I don't think, I see
                —not what I think,
blank face, forgetfulness,
the radiant void.
I lose my shadow,
                I move
through impalpable forests,
quick sculptures of the wind,
endless things,
            filed defiles,
I move,
        my steps
                dissolve
into a space that evaporates
into thoughts I don't think.


you fall from your body to your shadow *not there but in my eyes*
in an unmoving falling of waterfall *sky and earth joining*
you fall from your shadow to your name *untouchable horizon*
you drop through your likenesses *I am your remoteness*
you fall from your name to your body *the furthest point of seeing*
in a present that never ends *imaginings of sand*
you fall in your stirring *scattered fables of wind*
overflowing my body *I am the stela of your erosion*
you divide yourself up like speech *space a quartered god*
you divide me into your divisions *thought the altar and knife*
belly theater of blood *axis of the solstices*
arboreal ivy firebrand tongue of coolness *the firmament is*
                        *male and female*
the earth tremor of your buttocks *the testimony of solar testicles*
rain of your heels on my back *thought phallus word womb*
jaguar eye in the eyelash thicket *space is body sign thought*
the flesh-colored cleft in the brambles *always two*
                    *syllables in love*

the black lips of the prophetess *O r a c l e*
whole in each part you divide yourself *spirals*
                                        *transfigurations*
the bodies of the instant are your body *time world is body*
thought dream incarnated *seen touched dissolved*

observed by my ears              *unfolding horizon of music*
sniffled by my eyes              *bridge hung between color and smell*
caressed by my scent             *aroma nakedness in the hands of air*
heard by my tongue               *canticle of flavors*
eaten by my touch                *feast of mist*

to inhabit your name             *to depopulate your body*
to fall in your shriek with you  *house of the wind*

> The unreality of the watched
> makes the watching real.

                    In the center
       of the world of the body of the spirit
       the cleft                   the splendor
                        No
       In the whirlpool of disappearances
       the whirlwind of appearances
                        Yes
              The tree of names
                                        No
       is a word
                Yes
       is a word
                they are air nothing
       they are
                this insect
       fluttering among the lines
       of an unfinished
                        unfinishable
                        page

Thought
        fluttering
among these words
                They are
your footsteps in the next room
the birds that return
The neem tree that protects us
                        protects them
Its branches mute thunder
douse lightning
In its foliage the drought drinks water
They are
        this night
                (this music)
Watch it flow
                between your breasts
falling on your belly
                white and black
nocturnal spring
                jasmine and crow's wing
tabla and sitar
                No and Yes
together
        two syllables in love

If the world is real
                the word is unreal
If it is real the word
                the world
is the cleft the splendor the whirl
No
    the disappearances and the appearances
                                Yes
the tree of names
                Real unreal
are words
        air they are nothing
Speech
        unreal
makes silence real

                    Being still
        is a strand of language
                              Silence
seal
    scintilla
                    on the forehead
on the lips
                    before it evaporates
Appearances and disappearances
Reality and its resurrections
Silence rests in speech


The spirit
is an invention of the body
The body
is an invention of the world
The world
is an invention of the spirit
No                              Yes
    unreality of the watched
transparency is all that remains
Your footsteps in the next room
the green thunder
                    ripens
in the foliage of the sky
                    You are naked
like a syllable
                    like a flame
an island of flames
passion of compassionate coals
The world
                    bundle of your images
drowned in music
                    Your body
spilled on my body
                        seen
dissolved
            makes the watching real

*Delhi, 23 July–25 September, 1966*                    [E.W.]


                                                    91

# The Grove

*For Pere Gimferrer*

Enormous and solid
                    but swaying,
beaten by the wind
                    but chained,
murmur of a million leaves
against my window.
                    Riot of trees,
surge of dark green sounds.
                        The grove,
suddenly still,
            is a web of fronds and branches.
But there are flaming spaces
                        and, fallen into these meshes,
—restless,
        breathing—
is something violent and resplendent,
an animal swift and wrathful,
a body of light among the leaves:
                        the day.

To the left, above the wall,
                        more idea than color,
a bit of sky and many clouds,
                        a tile-blue basin
bordered by big, crumbling rocks,
                        sand cast down
into the funnel of the grove.
                        In the middle
thick drops of ink
                spattered
on a sheet of paper inflamed by the west;
it's black, there, almost entirely,
                        in the far southeast,
where the horizon breaks down.
                        The bower

92

turns copper, shines.
                        Three blackbirds
pass through the blaze and reappear,
                                    unharmed,
in the empty space: neither light nor shade.
                                        Clouds
on the way to their dissolution.

Lights are lit in the houses.
The sky gathers in the window.
                            The patio
enclosed in its four walls
                        grows more and more secluded.
Thus it perfects its reality.
                        And now the trash can,
the empty flower pot,
                    on the blind cement
contain nothing but shadows.
                            Space closes
over itself.
            Little by little the names petrify.

                                                [E.B.]


# Immemorial landscape

*For José de la Colina*


Airily flutters
                slips
among branches    trunks    poles
lazily
      hovers over
the high electric fruit
it falls
        aslant
                now blue
on the other snow

                    Made
of the same immaterial as shadow
it casts no shadow
                    As dense
as silence
            this snow
is snow, but it burns


                    Headlights
drill quick tunnels
                    collapsed
in a moment
                Night
riddled
        grows inward
grows night
                Obstinate cars
go by
        all
in different directions
to the same destination


                    One day
the streetlights will explode
from their iron stalks
                    One day
the bellowing river of engines
will be choked
                    One day
these houses will be hills
once more
                the wind in the stones
will talk only to itself
                        Aslant
among the shadows
                        unshadow
will fall
        almost blue
on the earth
                The same as tonight
the million year old snow                                    [E.W.]


94

# Trowbridge Street

I

Sun throughout the day
                    Cold throughout the sun
Nobody on the streets
                    parked cars
Still no snow
                but wind wind
A red tree
            still burns
in the chilled air
Talking to it I talk to you


2

I am in a room abandoned by language
You are in another identical room
Or we both are
on a street your glance has depopulated
The world
imperceptibly comes apart
                            Memory
decayed beneath our feet
I am stopped in the middle of this
unwritten line


3

Doors open and close by themselves
                            Air
enters and leaves our house
                            Air
talks to itself talking to you
                            Air
nameless in the endless corridor

Who knows who is on the other side?
                                        Air
turns and turns in my empty skull
                                    Air
turns to air everything it touches
                                    Air
with air-fingers scatters everything I say
I am the air you don't see
I can't open your eyes
                            I can't close the door
The air has turned solid


4

This hour has the shape of a pause
This pause has your shape
You have the shape of a fountain made
not of water but of time
My pieces bob
at the jet's tip
what I was    am    still am not
My life is weightless
                            The past thins out
The future    a little water in your eyes


5

Now you have a bridge-shape
Our room navigates beneath your arches
From your railing we watch us pass
You ripple with wind    more light than body
The sun on the other bank
                                    grows upside-down
Its roots buried deep in the sky
We could hide ourselves in its foliage
Build a bonfire with its branches
The day is habitable

The cold has immobilized the world
Space is made of glass
                              Glass made of air
The lightest sounds build
quick sculptures
Echoes multiply and disperse them
Maybe it will snow
The burning tree quivers
surrounded now by night
Talking to it I talk to you

[E.W.]

# Objects & apparitions

*For Joseph Cornell*

Hexahedrons of wood and glass,
scarcely bigger than a shoebox,
with room in them for night and all its lights.

Monuments to every moment,
refuse of every moment, used:
cages for infinity.

Marbles, buttons, thimbles, dice,
pins, stamps, and glass beads:
tales of the time.

Memory weaves, unweaves the echoes:
in the four corners of the box
shadowless ladies play a hide-and-seek.

Fire buried in the mirror,
water sleeping in the agate:
solos of Jenny Colonne and Jenny Lind.

"One has to commit a painting," said Degas,
"the way one commits a crime." But you constructed
boxes where things hurry away from their names.

Slot machine of visions,
condensation flask for conversations,
hotel of crickets and constellations.

Minimal, incoherent fragments:
the opposite of History, creator of ruins,
out of your ruins you have made creations.

Theater of the spirits:
objects putting the laws
of identity through hoops.

"Grand Hotel de la Couronne": in a vial,
the three of clubs and, very surprised,
Thumbelina in gardens of reflection.

A comb is a harp strummed by the glance
of a little girl
born dumb.

The reflector of the inner eye
scatters the spectacle:
God all alone above an extinct world.

The apparitions are manifest,
their bodies weigh less than light,
lasting as long as this phrase lasts.

Joseph Cornell: inside your boxes
my words became visible for a moment.

[E.B.]

# Return

*For José Alvarado*

> *It's better not to go back to the village,*
> *the subverted paradise silent.*
> *in the shatter of shrapnel.*
> Ramón López Velarde

Voices at the corner's turn
                voices
through the sun's spread hand
                    almost liquid
shadow and light
              The carpenter whistles
the iceman whistles
                 three ash trees
whistling in the plaza
               The invisible
foliage of sounds growing
rising up
        Time
stretched to dry on the rooftops
I am in Mixcoac
              Letters rot
in the mailboxes
              The bougainvillea
against the wall's white lime
                    flattened by the sun
a stain a purple
             passionate calligraphy
written by the sun
I am walking back
              back to what I left
or to what left me
             Memory
edge of the abyss
            balcony
over the void
             I walk and do not move forward
I am surrounded by city

                    I lack air
lack body
            lack
the stone that is pillow and slab
the grass that is cloud and water
Spirit flickers
                    Noon
pounding fist of light
To collapse in an office
                            or onto the pavement
to end up in a hospital
                            the pain of dying like that
isn't worth the pain
                    I look back
that passerby
                    nothing now but mist

Germination of nightmares
infestation of leprous images
in the belly brains lungs
in the genitals of the college and the temple
in the movie houses
                    desire's ghost population
in the meeting-places of here and there
this and that
            in the looms of language
in memory and its mansions
teeming clawed tusked ideas
swarms of reasons shaped like knives
in the catacombs in the plaza
in the hermit's well
in the bed of mirrors and in the bed of razors
in the sleepwalking sewers
in the objects in the store window
seated on a throne of glances

The vegetation of disaster
ripens beneath the ground
                            They are burning
millions and millions of old notes

in the Bank of Mexico
                    On corners and plazas
on the wide pedestals of the public squares
the Fathers of the Civic Church
a silent conclave of puppet buffoons
neither eagles nor jaguars
                    buzzard lawyers
locusts
        wings of ink    sawing mandibles
ventriloquist coyotes
                    peddlers of shadows
beneficent satraps
                the cacomistle    thief of hens
the monument to the Rattle and its snake
the altar to the mauser and the machete
the mausoleum of the epauletted cayman
rhetoric sculpted in phrases of cement

Paralytic architecture
                    stranded districts
rotting municipal gardens
                        mounds of saltpeter
deserted lots
            camps of urban nomads
ants' nests worm-farms
                    cities of the city
thoroughfares of scars
                    alleys of living flesh
Funeral Parlor
            by a window display of coffins
*whores*
    *pillars of vain night*
                At dawn
in the drifting bar
                the enormous mirror thaws
the solitary drinkers
contemplate the dissolution of their faces
The sun rises from its bed of bones
The air is not air
                it strangles without arms or hands

Dawn rips the curtains
                            City
heap of broken words


                    Wind
on the dusty corners
                        turns the papers
Yesterday's news
                    more remote
than a cuneiform tablet smashed to bits
Cracked scriptures
                        languages in pieces
the signs were broken
                        atl tlachinolli
                        burnt water      was split
There is no center
                        plaza of congregation and consecration
there is no axis
                    the years dispersed
horizons disbanded
                        They have branded the city
on every door
                    on every forehead
                                the $ sign


We are surrounded
                        I have gone back to where I began
Did I win or lose?
                    (*You ask*
*what laws rule "success" and "failure"?*
*The songs of the fishermen float up*
*from the unmoving riverbank*
                        Wang Wei to the Prefect Chang
from his cabin on the lake
                        But I don't want
an intellectual hermitage
in San Angel or Coyoacán)
                        All is gain
if all is lost
                    I walk toward myself


102

toward the plaza
                    Space is within
it is not a *subverted paradise*
                              it is a pulse-beat of time
Places are confluences
                    flutters of beings
in an instantaneous space
                         Wind whistles
in the ash tree
              fountains
almost liquid light and shadow
                              voices of water
shine   flow   are lost
                    a bundle of reflections
left in my hands
                I walk without moving forward
We never arrive
                Never reach where we are
Not the past
            the present is untouchable

                                        [E.W.]


# In the middle of this phrase . . .


I am not at the crest of the world.
                              The moment
is not the stylite's pillar,
                    time
doesn't rise from my feet,
                         doesn't burst
in my skull in a silent black explosion,
illumination the same as blindness.
I am on the sixth floor,
                    I am
in a cage hung from time.

                                        103

Sixth floor:
          clatter and surf,
battle of metals,
                    glasshatter,
engines with a rage now human.
                                        The night
is a disjointed murmur,
                    a body
self-embraced, tearing itself apart.
                              Blind,
fumbling to bind its pieces,
                    it gathers
its broken names and scatters them.
With lopped fingers
the city touches itself in dreams.


I am not at the crossroads:
                    to choose
is to go wrong.
          I am
in the middle of this phrase.
                         Where will it take me?
Rumbling tumble,
          data and date,
my birthfall:
          calendar dismembered
in the hollows of my memory.
I am the sack of my shadows.


                         Descent
to the slack breasts of my mother.
Wrinkled hills,
          swabbed lava,
sobbing fields,
          saltpeter meals.
Two workmen open the pit.
                    Crumbled
mouth of cement and brick.
The wracked box appears:
                    through the loose planks

the pearl-gray hat,
                    the pair of shoes,
the black suit of a lawyer.
                              Bones, buttons, rags:
sudden heap of dust
                    at the feet of the light.
Cold, *unused light*,
                    almost sleeping,
dawn light,
          just down from the hills,
shepherdess of the dead.
                         That which was my father
fits in that canvas sack
                         a workman hands me
as my mother crosses herself.
                              Before it ends
the vision scatters:
                    I am in the middle,
hung in a cage,
              hung in an image.
The beginning drifts off,
                         the end vanishes.
There is neither start nor finish:
                                  I am in the pause,
I neither end nor begin,
                        what I say
has neither hands nor feet.
                           I turn around in myself
and always find
               the same names,
the same faces,
              and never find myself.
My history is not mine:
                       a syllable from that broken phrase
the city in its circular fever
                              repeats and repeats.


City, my city,
             affronted stela,
dishonored stone,
                name spat out.

Your story is History:
                    fate
masked as freedom,
                    errant,
orbitless star,
                    a game
we all play without knowing the rules,
a game that no one wins,
                              a game without rules,
the whim of a speculative god,
                              a man
turned into a stuttering god.
                              Our oracles
are aphasic speech.
                    Our prophets
seers with glasses.
                    History:
coming and going
                    without beginning
                              without end.
No one has gone there,
                    no one
has drunk from the fountain
                    no one
has opened the stone eyelids of time,
                              no one
has heard the first word,
                              no one will hear the last,
the mouth that speaks it talks to itself,
                              no one
has gone down in the pit of the universes,
                              no one
has returned from the dungheap of the suns.


                    History:
dump and rainbow.
                    Scale
to the high terraces:
                    seven notes
dissolved in clarity.
                    Shadowless words.

We didn't hear them, we denied them,
                              we said they don't exist:
we were content with noise
                    Sixth floor:
I am in the middle of this phrase:
                              where
will it take me?
                    Mangled language.
Poet: gardener of epitaphs.

                                        [E.W.]


# The petrifying petrified


Deadland
          Shadeadland cactideous nopalopolis
bonéstony dushty mockedmire
                              empty socket
petrified fire
              the sun did not drink the lake
the earth did not absorb it
                              the water did not vanish into the air
men were the executors of the dust
wind
      swirled in the cold bed of fire
wind
      chanted litanies of drought
in the tomb of water
                    wind
broken knife in the worn crater
                              wind
saltpeter whisper


              The sun
solaortasoul centrotal soldonage
                              split

the word that came down in tongues of fire
                                        smashed
the account and the count of the years
the chant of the days
                        was a rain of scrap iron
slagheap of words
                        sand primers
crushed screams
                        hoofmuz zlebridlehar nessbit
whinning waning Cains
                        Abels in rubble
partisan assassins
                        pagan pedagogues
slick crooks
            the woofs of the one-eyed dog
guide of the dead
                        lost
in the coils of the Navel of the Moon


Valley of Mexico
                        lips in eclipse
lava slobber
            Rage's rotten throne
obstinate obsidian
                        petrified
petrifying
            Rage
                broken tower
tall as a scream
                        smeared breasts
tense brow
            greendry bloodsnot
                                Rage
nailed in a wound
                        ragerazor gazeblade
on a land of tines and spines

                    Circus of mountains
theater of clouds
                    table of noon
mat of the moon
                    garden of planets
drum of rain
                    balcony of breezes
seat of the sun
                    ball-game of the constellations
Bursting images
                    impaled images
the lopped hand leaps
                            the uprooted tongue leaps
the sliced breasts leap
                            the guillotined penis
over and over in the dust over and over
                                    in the courtyard
they trim the tree of blood
                            the intelligent tree


The dust of stuffed images
                            The Virgin
crown of snakes
                    The Flayed
The Felled-by-Arrows
                            The Crucified
The Hummingbird
                    winged spark
flowerbrand
                    The Flame
who speaks with words of water
                                    Our Lady
breasts of wine and belly of bread
                                    oven
where the dead burn and the living bake
The Spider
                    daughter of air
in her house of air
                    spins light

spins centuries and days
                    The Rabbit
wind
       carved in the mirror of the moon


                                    Images buried
in the eye of the dog of the dead
                            fallen
in the overgrown well of origins
                                whirlwinds of reflections
in the stone theater of memory
                            images
whirling in the circus of the empty eye
                                ideas
of red brown green
                        swarms of flies
ideas ate the deities
                        deities
became ideas
                great bladders full of bile
the bladders burst
                    the idols exploded
putrefaction of the deities
                            the sanctuary was a dungheap
the dungheap a nursery
                            armed ideas sprouted
ideolized ideodeities
                            sharpened syllogisms
cannibal deities
                    ideas idotic as deities
rabid dogs
            dogs in love with their own vomit


We have dug up Rage
The amphitheater of the genital sun is a dungheap
The fountain of lunar water is a dungheap
The lovers' park is a dungheap
The library is a nest of killer rats

110

The university is a muck full of frogs
The altar is Chanfalla's swindle
The brains are stained with ink
The doctors dispute in a den of thieves
The businessmen
fast hands   slow thoughts
officiate in the graveyard
The dialecticians exalt the subtlety of the rope
The casuists sprinkle thugs with holy water
nursing violence with dogmatic milk
The idée fixe gets drunk with its opposite
The juggling ideologist
                    sharpener of sophisms
in his house of truncated quotations and assignations
plots Edens for industrious eunuchs
forest of gallows   paradise of cages
            Stained images
         spit on the origins
      future jailers      present leeches
      affront the living body of time
         We have dug up Rage


On the chest of Mexico
                    tablets written by the sun
stairway of the centuries
                    spiral terrace of wind
the disinterred dances
                    anger panting thirst
the blind in combat beneath the noon sun
                              thirst panting anger
beating each other with rocks
                    the blind are beating each other
the men are crushing
                    the stones are crushing
within there is a water we drink
                         bitter water
water whetting thirst

            Where is the other water?

                              [E.W.]

# San Ildefonso nocturne

I

In my window night
                    invents another night,
another space:
                    carnival convulsed
in a square yard of blackness.
                              Momentary
confederations of fire,
                       nomadic geometries,
errant numbers.
              From yellow to green to red,
the spiral unwinds.
                   Window:
magnetic plate of calls and answers,
high-voltage calligraphy,
false heaven/hell of industry
on the changing skin of the moment.


Sign-seeds:
           the night shoots them off,
they rise,
          bursting above,
                          fall
still burning
             in a cone of shadow,
                                  reappear,
rambling sparks,
                syllable-clusters,
spinning flames
               that scatter,
                             smithereens once more.
The city invents and erases them.

I am at the entrance to a tunnel.
These phrases puncture time.
Perhaps I am that which waits at the end of the tunnel.
I speak with eyes closed.
                              Someone
has planted
                a forest of magnetic needles
                in my eyelids,
                              someone
guides the thread of these words.
                              The page
has become an ants' nest.
                         The void
has settled at the pit of my stomach.
                                   I fall
endlessly through that void.
                              I fall without falling.
My hands are cold,
                   my feet cold,
—but the alphabets are burning, burning.
                                        Space
constructs and deconstructs itself.
                              The night insists,
the night touches my forehead,
                            touches my thoughts.
What does it want?


2

Empty streets, squinting lights.
                           On a corner,
the ghost of a dog
                  searches the garbage
for a spectral bone.
                    Uproar in a nearby patio:
cacophonous cockpit.
                    Mexico, circa 1931.
Loitering sparrows,
                   a flock of children
builds a nest
             of unsold newspapers.

In the desolation
             the streetlights invent
unreal pools of yellowish light.
                          Apparitions:
time splits open:
                  a lugubrious, lascivious clatter of heels,
beneath *a sky of soot*
                   *the flash of a skirt.*
*C'est la mort—ou la morte . . .*
                     The indifferent wind
pulls torn posters from the walls.

At this hour,
             the red walls of San Ildefonso
are black, and they breathe:
                          sun turned to time,
time turned to stone,
                   stone turned to body.
These streets were once canals.
                        In the sun,
the houses were silver:
                     city of mortar and stone,
moon fallen in the lake.
                     Over the filled canals
and the buried idols
                  the *criollos* erected
another city
          —not white, but red and gold—
idea turned to space, tangible number.
                               They placed it
at the crossroads of eight directions,
                            its doors
open to the invisible:
                    heaven and hell.

Sleeping district.
                 We walk through galleries of echoes,
past broken images:
               our history.
Hushed nation of stones.
                      Churches,

dome-growths,
                    their facades
petrified gardens of symbols.
                              Shipwrecked
in the spiteful proliferation of dwarf houses:
humiliated palaces,
                    fountains without water,
affronted frontispieces.
                        Cumuli,
insubstantial madrepore,
                         accumulate
over the ponderous bulks,
                          conquered
not by the weight of the years
but by the infamy of the present.


                              Zócalo Plaza,
vast as the earth:
                   diaphanous space,
court of echoes.
                There,
with Alyosha K and Julien S,
                             we devised bolts of lightning
against the century and its cliques.
                                     The wind of thought
carried us away,
                 the verbal wind,
the wind that plays with mirrors,
                                  master of reflections,
builder of cities of air,
                          geometries
hung from the thread of reason.


Shut down for the night,
                         the yellow trolleys,
giant worms.
            S's and Z's:
a crazed auto, insect with malicious eyes.
                                          Ideas,
fruits within an arm's reach,

like stars,
burning.
The girandola is burning,
the adolescent dialogue,
the scorched hasty frame.
The bronze fist
of the towers beats
12 times.
Night
bursts into pieces,
gathers them by itself,
and becomes one, intact.
We disperse,
not there in the plaza with its dead trains,
but here,
on this page: petrified letters.


3

The boy who walks through this poem,
between San Ildefonso and the Zócalo,
is the man who writes it:
this page too
is a ramble through the night.
Here the friendly ghosts
become flesh,
ideas dissolve.

Good, we wanted good:
to set the world right.
We didn't lack integrity:
we lacked humility.
What we wanted was not innocently wanted.
Precepts and concepts,
the arrogance of theologians,
to beat with a cross,
to institute with blood,
to build the house with bricks of crime,
to declare obligatory communion.

                              Some
became secretaries to the secretary
to the General Secretary of the Inferno.
                              Rage
became philosophy,
                 its drivel has covered the planet.
Reason came down to earth,
took the form of a gallows
                     —and is worshiped by millions.
Circular plot:
              we have all been,
in the Great Flayhouse of the World,
judge, executioner, victim, witness,
                              we have all
given false testimony
                 against the others
and against ourselves.
                      And the most vile: we
were the public that applauded or yawned in its seats.
The guilt that knows no guilt,
                              innocence
was the greatest guilt.
                  Each year was a mountain of bones.


Conversions, retractions, excommunications,
reconciliations, apostasies, recantations,
the zig-zag of the demonolatries and the androlatries,
bewitchments and aberrations:
my history.
          Are they the histories of an error?
History is the error.
                 Further than dates,
closer than names,
                 truth is that
which history scorns:
                 the everyday
—everyone's anonymous heartbeat,
                              the unique
beat of every one—
                 the unrepeatable

everyday, identical to all days.
                                        Truth
is the base of time without history.
                                        The weight
of the weightless moment:
                        a few stones in the sun
seen long ago,
                today return,
stones of time that are also stone
beneath this sun of time,
sun that comes from a dateless day,
                                        sun
that lights up these words,
                        sun of words
that burn out when they are named.
                                Suns, words, stones,
burn and burn out:
                        the moment burns them
without burning.
                Hidden, immobile, untouchable,
the present—not its presences—is always.

Between seeing and making,
                        contemplation or action,
I chose the act of words:
                        to make them, to inhabit them,
to give eyes to the language.
                                Poetry is not truth:
it is the resurrection of presences,
                                history
transfigured in the truth of undated time.
Poetry,
        like history, is made;
                        poetry,
like truth, is seen.
                        Poetry:
                        incarnation
of the-sun-on-the-stones in a name,
                                dissolution
of the name in a beyond of stones.

118

Poetry,
          suspension bridge between history and truth,
is not a path toward this or that:
                              it is to see
the stillness in motion,
                    change
in stillness.
               History is the path:
it goes nowhere,
                    we all walk it,
truth is to walk it.
                    We neither go nor come:
we are in the hands of time.
                         Truth:
to know ourselves,
               from the beginning,
                              hung.
Brotherhood over the void.


4

Ideas scatter,
          the ghosts remain:
truth of the lived and suffered.
An almost empty taste remains:
                              time
—shared fury—
                    time
—shared oblivion—
                    in the end transfigured
in memory and its incarnations.
                         What remains is
time as portioned body: language.

In the window,
          battle simulacrum:
the commercial sky of advertisements
                              flares up, goes out.

Behind,
          barely visible,
                    the true constellations.
Among the water towers, antennas, rooftops,
a liquid column,
                    more mental than corporeal,
a waterfall of silence:
                    the moon.
                              Neither phantom nor idea:
once a goddess,
          today an errant clarity.
My wife sleeps.
          She too is a moon,
a clarity that travels
                    not between the reefs of the clouds,
but between the rocks and wracks of dreams:
she too is a soul.
          She flows below her closed eyes,
a silent torrent
          rushing down
from her forehead to her feet,
                    she tumbles within,
bursts out from within,
                    her heartbeats sculpt her,
traveling through herself
                    she invents herself,
inventing herself
          she copies it,
she is an arm of the sea
                    between the islands of her breasts,
her belly a lagoon
                    where darkness and its foliage
grow pale,
          she flows through her shape,
rises,
     falls,
          scatters in herself,
                    ties

herself to her flowing,
                    disperses in her form:
she too is a body.
                    Truth
is the swell of a breath
and the visions closed eyes see:
the palpable mystery of the person.


The night is at the point of running over.
                              It grows light.
The horizon has become aquatic.
                              To rush down
from the heights of this hour:
                              will dying
be a falling or a rising,
                    a sensation or a cessation?
I close my eyes,
          I hear in my skull
the footsteps of my blood,
                    I hear
time pass through my temples.
                    I am still alive.
The room is covered with moon.
                    Woman:
fountain in the night.
          I am bound to her quiet flowing.
                                        [E.W.]



121

# A draft of shadows

*Fair seed-time had my soul, and I grew up*
*Foster'd alike by beauty and by fear . . .*
W.W. *The Prelude* (I, 265-266)

Heard by the soul, footsteps
in the mind more than shadows,
shadows of thought more than footsteps
through the path of echoes
that memory invents and erases:
without walking they walk
over this present, bridge
slung from one letter to the next.
Like drizzle on embers,
footsteps within me step
toward places that turn to air.
Names: they vanish
in a pause between two words.
The sun walks through the rubble
of what I'm saying; the sun
razes the places as they dawn,
hesitantly, on this page;
the sun opens my forehead,
                         balcony
perched within me.


                         I drift away from myself,
following this meandering phrase,
this path of rocks and goats.
Words glitter in the shadows,
and the black tide of syllables
covers the page, sinking
its ink roots
in the subsoil of language.
From my forehead I set out
toward a noon the size of time.

A banyan's centuries of assault
on the vertical patience of a wall
last less than this brief
bifurcation of thought:
the seen and the foreseen.
Neither here not there,
through that frontier of doubt,
crossed only by glimmers and mirages,
where language recants,
I travel toward myself.
The hour is a crystal ball.
I enter an abandoned patio:
apparition of an ash tree.
Green exclamations,
wind in the branches.
On the other side, the void.
Inconclusive patio, threatened
by writing and its uncertainties.
I walk among the images
of an eye that has lost its memory.
I am one of its images.
The ash tree, sinuous liquid flame,
is a murmur rising
till it becomes a speaking tower.
Garden turned to scrub:
its fever invents creatures
the mythologies later copy.
Adobe, lime and time:
the dark walls that are and are not.
Infinitesimal wonders in their cracks:
the phantom mushroom, vegetable Mithridates,
the newt and its fiery breath.
I am inside the eye: the well where,
from the beginning, a boy is falling,
the well where I recount the time
spent falling from the beginning,
the well of the account of my account,
where the water rises
and my shadow falls.

Patio, wall, ash tree, well,
dissolve into a clarity in the form of a lake.
A foliage of transparency
grows on its shore. Fortunate
rhyme of peaks and pyramids,
the landscape unfolds
in the abstract mirror of the architecture.
Scarcely drawn,
a kind of horizontal comma ( ⌣ )
between the earth and sky:
a solitary canoe.
The waves speak Nahuatl.
A sign flies across the heights.
Perhaps it is a date, conjunction of destinies:
bundle of reeds, the omen of the pyre.
The flint and the cross, keys of blood:
have they ever opened the doors of death?
The western light lingers,
raising symmetrical fires
across the rug, changing
this scarlet book I skim
(engravings: volcanoes, temples,
and the feathered cloak stretched over the water:
Tenochtitlán soaked in blood)
into a chimerical flame.
The books on the shelf now are embers
the sun stirs with its red hands.
My pencil rebels against dictation.
The lake is eclipsed
by the writing that names it.
I fold the page. Whispers:
they are watching me
from the foliage of the letters.


                My memory: a puddle.
A muddy mirror: where was I?
My eyes, without anger or pity,
look me in the eye
from the troubled waters

of the puddle my words evoke.
I don't see with my eyes: words
are my eyes. We live among names;
that which has no name
still does not exist:
*Adam of mud,*
not a clay doll: a metaphor.
To see the world is to spell it.
Mirror of words: where was I?
My words watch me from the puddle
of my memory. Syllables of water
shine in a grove of reflections,
stranded clouds, bubbles above a bottom
that changes from gold to rust.
Rippling shadows, flashes, echoes,
the writing not of signs, but of murmurs.
My eyes are thirsty. The puddle is Stoic:
the water is for reading, not drinking.
In the sun of the high plains the puddles evaporate.
Only some faithless dust remains,
and a few intestate relics.
Where was I?


                    I am where I was:
within the indecisive walls
of that same patio of words.
Abd al-Rahman, Pompeii, Xicontencatl,
battles on the Oxus or on top of the wall
with Ernesto and Guillermo. Thousands of leaves,
dark green sculpture of whispers,
cage of the sun and the hummingbird's flash:
the primordial fig tree,
leafy chapel of polymorphous,
diverse and perverse rituals.
Revelations and abominations:
the body and its interwoven languages,
knot of phantoms touched by thought
and dissolved with a touch,

pillory of blood, idée fixe
nailed to my forehead.
Desire is the master of ghosts,
desire turns us into ghosts.
We are vines of air on trees of wind,
a cape of flames
invented and devoured by flame.
The crack in the tree trunk:
sex, seal, serpentine passage
closed to the sun and to my eyes,
open to the ants.


That crack was the portico
of the furthest reaches of the seen and thought:
—there, inside, tides are green,
blood is green, fire green,
green stars burn in the black grass:
the green music of elytra
in the fig tree's pristine night;
—there, inside, fingertips are eyes,
to touch is to see, glances touch,
eyes hear smells;
—there, inside is outside,
it is everywhere and nowhere,
things are themselves and others,
imprisoned in an icosahedron
there is a music weaver beetle
and another insect unweaving
the syllogisms the spider weaves,
hanging from the threads of the moon;
—there, inside, space
is an open hand, a mind
that thinks shapes, not ideas,
shapes that breathe, walk, speak, transform
and silently evaporate;
—there, inside, land of woven echoes,
a slow cascade of light drops
between the lips of the crannies:
light is water; water, diaphanous time

where eyes wash their images;
—there, inside, cables of desire
mimic the eternities of a second
the mind's electric current
turns on, turns off, turns on,
flaming resurrections
of a charred alphabet;
—there is no school there, inside,
it is always the same day, the same night always,
time has not yet been invented,
the sun has not grown old,
this snow is the same as grass,
always and never the same,
it has never rained, it always rains,
everything is being, and has never been,
a nameless people of sensations,
names that search for a body,
pitiless transparencies, cages of clarity
where identity cancels itself in its likenesses,
difference in its contradictions.
The fig tree, its lies and its wisdom:
wonders of the earth
—trustworthy, punctual, redundant—
and the conversations with ghosts.
An apprenticeship with the fig tree:
talking with the living and the dead.
And with myself.


           The year's procession:
changes that are repetitions.
The way and the weight of time.
Dawn: more than light,
a vapor of clarity
changed into gravid drops
on the windowpanes and on the leaves:
the world grows thin in these vibrating geometries
until it becomes the edge of a reflection.
The day buds, breaking out among the leaves,

spinning over itself,
surging, again incarnate,
from the vacuum into which it falls.
Time is filtered light.
The black fruit bursts
in the flesh-colored blossoms,
the broken branch leaks sour, milky sap.
The fig tree's metamorphosis:
burnt by autumn, transfigured by autumn's light.
It rises through diaphanous spaces,
a bare black virgin.
The sky is a revolving lapis lazuli:
its continents wheel *au ralenti*,
geographies without substance.
Flames in the snow of the clouds.
The afternoon turns to burnt honey.
Silent landslide of horizons:
light falls from the peaks,
shadow overflows the plain.


By the light of a lamp—night now
mistress of the house,
and the ghost of my grandfather
now master of the night—
I would penetrate silence,
bodiless body, time
without hours. Each night books,
transparent fever machines, raised within me
architectures built above an abyss.
A breath of the spirit creates them,
a blink of the eye tears them down.
I gathered wood with the others,
and wept from the smoke
of the horse-tamer's pyre;
I wandered on the floating grove
the turbulent green Tagus dragged along:
the liquid thicket curling
behind the fleeing Galatea;
I saw, in bunches of grapes, the shades clustered

to drink the blood in the pit:
*better to live as a peasant,*
*breaking clods of dirt for a dog's ration,*
*than to rule this pale nation of the dead;*
I was thirsty, I saw demons in the Gobi;
I swam in the grotto with the siren
(and later, in the cathartic dream,
*fendendo i drappi, e mostravami 'l ventre,*
*quel mi svegliò col puzzo che n'uscia*);
I engraved on my imaginary tomb:
*Do not move this stone*
*My only riches are bones:*
those memorable *freckled pears*
found in Villaurrutia's basket of words;
Carlos Garrote, eternal half-brother,
*God save you,* he cried, as he knocked me down,
and it was, in the mirrors of recurrent insomnia,
I myself who had wounded me;
Isis and Lucius the ass; Nemo and the squid;
and the books marked with the arms of Priapus,
read on diluvial afternoons,
body tense, eyes intent.
Names anchored in the bay
of my forehead: I write because the druid,
under the murmuring syllables of the hymn,
ilex planted deeply on the page,
gave me the branch of mistletoe, the spell
that makes words flow from stone.
Names accumulate their images,
images their vaporous
conjectural confederations.
Clouds and clouds, a phantom gallop
of clouds over the peaks
of my memory. Adolescence,
land of clouds.


The big house,
stranded in clogged time.
The plaza, the great trees

where the sun nestled,
the tiny church: its belfry
only reached their knees,
but its double tongue of metal
woke the dead.
Under the arcade, in military sheaves,
the cane, green lances,
sugar rifles;
at the portal, the magenta stall:
the coolness of water kept in the shade,
the ancestral palm-mats, knotted light,
and on the zinc counter
the miniature planets
fallen from the meridian tree,
sloes and mandarins,
yellow heaps of sweetness.
The years turn in the plaza,
a Catharine wheel,
and do not move.


                    My words,
speaking of the house, split apart.
Rooms and rooms inhabited
only by their ghosts,
only by the rancor of the elderly
inhabited. Families,
breeding-grounds for scorpions:
as they give ground glass to dogs
with their pittance, so they nourish us with their hates
and the doubtful ambition of being someone.
They also gave me bread, gave me time,
open spaces in the corners of the days,
backwaters to be alone with myself.
Child among tactiturn adults
and their terrifying childishness,
child in passageways with tall doors,
rooms with portraits,
dim brotherhoods of the departed,
child survivor

of mirrors with no memory
and their people of wind:
time and its incarnations
resolved in the simulacra of reflections.
In my house there were more dead than living.
My mother, a thousand-year-old girl,
mother of the world, my orphan,
self-sacrificing, ferocious, stubborn, provident,
titmouse, bitch, ant, wild boar,
love letter with spelling mistakes;
my mother: bread I'd slice
with her own knife each day.
Under the rain,
the ash trees taught me patience,
to sing facing the violent wind.
A virgin who talked in her sleep, my aunt
taught me to see with eyes closed,
to see within, and through the wall;
my grandfather, to smile at defeat,
and for disasters: *in affliction, conviction.*
(This that I say is earth thrown over
your name: *let it rest softly.*)
Between vomit and thirst,
strapped to the rack of alcohol,
my father came and went through flames.
One evening of flies and dust,
we gathered, among the rails and crossties
of a railway station, his remains.
I could never talk to him.
I meet him now in dreams,
that blurred country of the dead.
We always speak of other things.
As the house crumbled, I grew.
I was (I am) grass,
weeds in anonymous trash.


                    Days,
like a free mind, an open book.

I was not multiplied by the envious mirrors
that turn men into things, things into numbers:
neither power nor gain. Nor sanctity either:
heaven for me soon became an uninhabited piece of sky,
an adorable and hollow beauty.
Sufficient and changing presence:
time and its epiphanies.
God did not talk to me from the clouds;
from the leaves of the fig tree
my body spoke to me, the bodies of my body.
Instantaneous incarnations:
afternoon washed by rain,
light just coming out from the water,
the feminine mist of plants,
skin stuck to my skin: succubus!
—as if time at last were to coincide
with itself, and I with it,
as if time and its two times
were one single time
that still was not time, a time
where always is *now* and anytime *always*,
as if I and my double were one
and I was no longer.
Pomegranate of the hour: I drank sun, I ate time.
Fingers of light would part the foliage.
Bees humming in my blood:
the white advent.
The shot flung me
to the loneliest shore. I was a stranger
in the vast ruins of the afternoon.
Abstract vertigo: I talked with myself,
I was double, time split apart.


Amazed at the moment's peak,
flesh became word—and the word fell.
To know exile on the earth, being earth,
is to know mortality. An open secret,
an empty secret with nothing inside:

there are no dead, there is only death, our mother.
The Aztecs knew it, the Greeks divined it:
water is fire, and in its passage
we are only flashes of flame.
Death is the mother of forms . . .
Sound, the blindman's cane of sense:
I write *death* and for a moment
I live within it. I inhabit its sound:
a pneumatic cube of glass,
vibrating on this page,
vanishing among its echoes.
Landscapes of words:
my eyes, reading, depopulate them.
It doesn't matter: my ears propagate them.
They breed there, in the indecisive
zones of language, the villages in the marsh.
They are amphibious creatures, they are words.
They pass from one element to another,
they bathe in fire, rest in the air.
They are from the other side.
I don't hear them: what do they say?
They don't say: they talk and talk.


      I leap from one story to another on a
suspension bridge of eleven syllables.
A body, living but intangible, the air
in all places always and in none.
It sleeps with open eyes,
it lies down in the grass and wakes up as dew,
it chases itself, talks to itself in tunnels,
is a bit that drills into mountains,
a swimmer in the rough seas of fire,
an invisible fountain of laments,
it lifts two oceans with a hand,
and walks through the streets, lost,
a word in limbo in search of meaning,
air that vanishes into air.
And why do I say all this?
To say that, at high noon,

the air was populated with phantoms,
sun coined into wings,
weightless change, butterflies.
Night fell. On the terrace
the silenciary moon officiated.
A death's-head, messenger
of the souls, the enchanting
enchanted by the camelias
and the electric light, was,
over our heads, a fluttering
of opaque conjurations. *Kill it!*
the woman shouted
and burned it like a witch.
Then, with a fierce sigh, they crossed themselves.
Scattered light, Psyche . . .


                      Are there messengers? Yes,
space is a body tattooed with signs, the air
an invisible web of calls and answers.
Animals and things make languages,
through us the universe talks with itself.
We are a fragment—
accomplished in our unaccomplishment—
of its discourse. A coherent
and empty solipsism:
since the beginning of the beginning
what does it say? It says that it says us.
It says it to itself. *Oh madness of discourse,*
*that cause sets up with and against itself!*


From the moment's peak flung down
into an afternoon of sexual plants,
I discovered death.
And in death I discovered language.
The universe talks to itself,
but people talk to people:
there is history. Guillermo, Alfonso, Emilio:
the patio where we played was history,

it was history to play at death together.
The clouds of dust, the shouts, the tumbles:
gabble, not speech.
In the aimless give-and-take of things,
carried along by the revolutions of forms and times,
everyone battles with the others,
everyone rebels, blindly, against himself.
Thus, returning to their origin,
they pay for their injustice. (Anaximander)
The injustice of being: things suffer
one with the other and with themselves
for to be is the desire to be more,
to always be more than more.
To be time is the sentence; history, our punishment.
But it is also the proving-ground:
to see, in the blot of blood
on Veronica's cloth, the face
of another—always the other is our victim.
Tunnels, galleries of history:
is death the only exit?
The way out, perhaps, is toward within.
The purgation of language, history consuming itself
in the dissolution of pronouns:
not *I am* nor *I even more so*
but more being without I.
In the center of time, there is no more time,
but motion become fixity, a circle
canceled by its revolutions.


Noon:
the trees in the patio are green flames.
The crackling of the last embers
in the grass: stubborn insects.
Over the yellow meadows,
clarities: the glass footsteps of autumn.
A fortuitous meeting of reflections,
an ephemeral bird
enters the foliage of these letters.
The sun, in my writing, drinks the shadows.

Between the walls—not of stone,
but raised by memory—
a transitory grove:
reflective light among the trunks
and the breathing of the wind.
The bodiless god, the nameless god
whom we call by empty names—
by the names of the emptiness—
the god of time, the god that is time,
passes through the branches
that I write. Dispersion of clouds
above a neutral mirror:
in the dissipation of the images,
the soul already is, vacant, pure space.
Motion resolves in tranquility.
The sun insists, fastened
in the corolla of the absorbed hour.
Flame on the water-stalk
of the words that say it,
the flower is another sun.
Tranquility dissolves in itself. Time
elapses without elapse. It passes and stays. Perhaps
although we all pass, it neither passes nor stays:
there is a third state.


A third state:
being without being, empty plenitude,
hour without hours and the other names
with which it appears and vanishes
in the confluences of language.
Not the presence: its presentiment.
The names that name it say: *nothing*,
double-edged word, word between two hollows.
Its house, built on air
with bricks of fire and walls of water,
constructs and deconstructs and is the same
from the beginning. It is god:
it inhabits the names that deny it.

In the conversations with the fig tree
or in the pauses of speech,
in the conjuration of the images
against my closed eyelids,
in the delirium of the symmetries,
the quicksands of insomnia,
the dubious garden of memory,
or in the rambling paths,
it was the eclipse of the clarities.
It appeared in every form
of vanishing.


                Bodiless god,
my senses named it
in the languages of the body.
I wanted to name it
with a solar name,
a word without reverse.
I exhausted the dice box and *ars combinatoria*.
A rattle of dried seeds,
the broken letters of names:
we have crushed names,
we have scattered names,
we have dishonored names.
Since then, I have been in search of the name.
I followed a murmur of languages,
rivers between rocks
*color ferrigno* of these times.
Pyramids of bones, rotting-places of words:
our masters are garrulous and bloodthirsty.
I built with words and their shadows
a movable house of reflections,
a walking tower, edifice of wind.
Time and its combinations:
the years and the dead and the syllables,
different accounts from the same account.
Spiral of echoes, the poem
is air that sculpts itself and dissolves,
a fleeting allegory of true names.

At times the page breathes:
the swarm of signs, the errant
republics of sounds and senses,
in magnetic rotation
link and scatter
on the page.


　　　　　I am where I was:
I walk behind the murmur,
footsteps within me, heard with my eyes,
the murmur is in the mind, I am my footsteps,
I hear the voices that I think,
the voices that think me as I think them.
I am the shadow my words cast.

　　　　　　　　　　　　　　　[E.W.]


# Flame, speech


I read in a poem:
*to talk is divine.*
But the gods don't speak:
they make and unmake worlds
while men do the talking.
They play frightening games
without words.

The spirit descends,
loosening tongues,
but doesn't speak words:
it speaks fire.
Lit by a god,
language becomes
a prophecy
of flames and a tower
of smoke and collapse

138

of syllables burned:
ash without meaning.

The word of man
is the daughter of death.
We talk because we are mortal:
words are not signs, they are years.
Saying what they say,
the words we are saying
say time: they name us.
We are time's names.

To talk is human.

[M.S.]

# Sight, touch

*For Balthus*

Light holds between its hands
the white hill and black oaks,
the path that goes on,
the tree that stays;

light is a stone that breathes
by the sleepwalking river,
light: a girl stretching,
a dark bundle dawning;

light shapes the breeze in the curtains,
makes a living body from each hour,
enters the room and slips out,
barefoot, on the edge of a knife;

light is born a woman in a mirror,
naked under diaphanous leaves,
chained by a look,
dissolved in a wink;

it touches the fruit and the unbodied,
it is a pitcher from which the eye drinks clarities,
a flame cut in blossom, a candle watching
where the blackwinged butterfly burns;

light opens the folds of the sheets
and the creases of puberty,
glows in the fireplace, its flames become shadows
that climb the walls, yearning ivy;

light does not absolve or condemn,
is neither just or unjust,
light with impalpable hands raises
the buildings of symmetry;

light escapes through a passage of mirrors
and returns to light:
is a hand that invents itself,
an eye that sees itself in its own inventions.

Light is time reflecting on time.

[M.S.]

# Homage to Claudius Ptolemy

(PALATINE ANTHOLOGY 9.577)

I am a man: little do I last
and the night is enormous.
But I look up:
the stars write.
Unknowing I understand:
I too am written,
and at this very moment
someone spells me out.

[E.W.]

# Stars and cricket

        The sky's big.
Up there, worlds scatter.
        Persistent,
Unfazed by such a night,
        Cricket:
        Brace and bit.

[E.W.]

# Wind and water and stone

*For Roger Caillois*

The water hollowed the stone,
the wind dispersed the water,
the stone stopped the wind.
Water and wind and stone.

The wind sculpted the stone,
the stone is a cup of water,
the water runs off and is wind.
Stone and wind and water.

The wind sings in its turnings,
the water murmurs as it goes,
the motionless stone is quiet.
Wind and water and stone.

One is the other, and is neither:
among their empty names
they pass and disappear,
water and stone and wind.

[M.S.]

# Epitaph for no stone

Mixcoac was my village. Three nocturnal syllables,
a half-mask of shadow across a solar face.
Clouds of dust came and ate it.
I escaped and walked through the world.
My words were my house, air my tomb.

[E.W.]


# This side

*For Donald Sutherland*


There is light. We neither see nor touch it.
In its empty clarities rests
what we touch and see.
I see with my fingertips
what my eyes touch:
                        shadows, the world.
With shadows I draw worlds,
I scatter worlds with shadows.
I hear the light beat on the other side.

[E.W.]

# Author's notes

## OBSIDIAN BUTTERFLY

Obsidian butterfly: Itzpapálotl, goddess sometimes confused with Teteoinan, our mother, and Tonatzin. All of these female divinities were fused in the cult which, since the 16th century, has worshiped the Virgin of Guadalupe.

## SUN STONE

The well-known Aztec calendar measured the synodical period of the planet Venus—for the ancient Mexicans one of the manifestations of the god Quetzalcoatl, the Plumed Serpent. The calendar begins, as the poem does, at Day 4 Olín (Movement) and ends 584 days later at Day 4 Ehécatl (Wind), the conjunction of the planet and the sun: the end of a cycle and the beginning of another. *Sun stone* is composed of 584 lines of eleven syllables each.

## HAPPINESS IN HERAT

"Memories of a poet-saint": the Sufi mystic and theologian Hazrat Khwaja Abdullah Ansar. There is an almost withered tree in the garden which surrounds his tomb. Devotees drive iron nails into the tree to ward off the evil eye and to cure toothaches.

"the turquoise cupola": on the mausoleum of Gahar Shad, the wife of Shah Rakh, the son of Timur, Governor of Herat.

"the two and thirty signs": according to the Mahayana Sutras, certain signs appear on the bodies of Boddhisattvas (the future Buddhas), usually 32 in number. Nevertheless, the same texts insist on the illusory nature of these signs: what distinguishes a Boddhisattva from other beings is the absence of signs.

143

The mausoleums of the Lodi Dynasty (1451–1526) in Delhi.

VRINDABAN

One of the sacred cities of Hinduism, on the outskirts of Mathura. According to legend, Krishna spent his childhood and youth in the forest of Vrindaban, now a barren plain, producing wonders, seducing the cowgirls, and falling in love with Radha.

"sadhu": a wandering ascetic.

"blue tree": Krishna is blue and black, like the Mexican god Mixcóatl.

"Perhaps is a cleft stone/ He grasped the form of a woman": certain stones are symbols of the Great Goddess, particularly those whose form suggests a vulva (yoni).

"Gone gone": the expression "Gone gone to the Other Shore" occurs frequently in the Prajnaparamita Sutra. It means: knowledge has crossed over from this bank, the phenomenal world, to the other, Perfect Wisdom.

ON READING JOHN CAGE

The italicized quotations are from Cage's book, *A Year from Monday*.

"Nirvana is Samsara/ Samsara is not Nirvana": in Mahayana Buddhist literature we find the formula "Nirvana is Samsara, Samsara is Nirvana," which sums up one of the central ideas of the Madhyamika school: the ultimate identity of phenomenal (Samsara) and transcendental (Nirvana) reality. Both are merely aspects of the void (Sunyata), and true wisdom transcends their apparent duality. But the poem says something slightly different . . .

WIND FROM ALL COMPASS POINTS

"If we had the munitions/ You people would not be here": Mexican history schoolbooks attribute this statement to General Anaya when he surrendered the Plaza de Churubusco to

General Scott, the head of the U.S. troops that invaded Mexico in 1847.

Santo Domingo: the poem was written during the American intervention in the Dominican Republic.

"Tipoo Sultan planted the Jacobin tree": the facts referred to here are historical.

Datia: the palace-castle in the walled city of the same name, in Madhya Pradesh. Built on a black, craggy promontory it towers over the city and the plain. According to Fergusson, it is the finest example of palace architecture in the 17th century. Built by a prince pledged to the Emperor Jahangir, the castle was never inhabited, except by bats and snakes: its owner was assassinated before he could move in, and since then no one else has dared try.

"In a fig-leaf you sail": an allusion to the children's book, *Almendrita* ("Little Almond").


MAITHUNA

Maithuna: the erotic couples that cover the walls of certain Buddhist and Hindu temples; sexual union; the path of illumination, in Tantric Buddhism and Hinduism, through the conjunction of karuna (passion) and prajna (wisdom). Karuna is the masculine side of reality and prajna the feminine. Their union is sunyata, the void.

The seventh section of the poem is an imitation of Li Po.


SUNDAY ON THE ISLAND OF ELEPHANTA

The sculptures in the Shivaite caves of Elephanta (7th century) are among the most beautiful in Indian art. The reliefs represent scenes from the legends of Shiva and Parvati. The religious fervor of the Portuguese mutilated, but did not destroy, their beauty.


RETURN

"the pain of dying . . .": Masaoka Shiki (1867–1902).

"whores/pillars": "Crepúsculos de la ciudad II" [an untranslated early Paz poem].

"atl tlachinolli": a Nahuatl expression meaning "burnt (something)/water." The hieroglyph is often found on Aztec monuments. Alfonso Caso states that "water" also means blood, and that "burnt (something)" alludes to fire. The opposition of water and fire is a metaphor of cosmic war, modeled, in turn, on the wars between men. Cities and civilizations are founded on an image: water and fire was the metaphor of the foundation of the city of Mexico. It is an image of the cosmos and man as a vast contradictory unity.

Tragic vision: the cosmos is movement, and the axis of blood of that movement is man. After wandering for some centuries, the Mexica founded Mexico Tenochtitlán precisely in the place indicated in the auguries of their god Huitzilopochtli: the rock in the lake; on the rock, a nopal, the plant whose fruit symbolizes human hearts; on the nopal, an eagle, the solar bird that devours the red fruit; a snake; white water; trees and grass that were also white . . .


IN THE MIDDLE OF THIS PHRASE

"unused light": Fray Luis de Léon, "A Francisco de Salinas."


THE PETRIFYING PETRIFIED

"the one-eyed dog": Xólotl, the double of Quetzalcoatl; the god who, in penance, pulled out an eye and descended to the underworld in the form of a dog.

"navel of the moon": Mexico is a word composed of *metztli* (moon), *xictli* (navel) and *co* (place): the place of the navel of the moon; that is, in the navel of the lake of the moon, as the lake of Mexico was called.

Chanfalla: Cervantes, *El retablo de las maravillas.*


SAN ILDEFONSO NOCTURNE

"Sky of soot": Ramón López Velarde, "Dia 13."
"C'est la mort": Gérard de Nerval, "Artémis."


146

A DRAFT OF SHADOWS

[The Spanish title, "Pasado en claro," means "clean copy" (as in the preparation of a manuscript) but with the added resonance of "pasado" (past/passed) and "claro" (clear or bright, in all their uses). The English title is a collaborative invention.]


NOTE ON THE TRANSLATIONS

[As explained in the Introduction, the following changes have been made in the translations to correspond to Paz's revision of the Spanish text: "The Bird": one line deleted. "In Uxmal": the first poem replaced by another. "Riprap": an eighth poem added. "Hymn among the ruins": p. 23, lines 14–16 added. "The River": p. 29, lines 3–8 are a condensation and re-arrangement of the earlier version. "Wind from all compass points": p. 70, lines 29–34 added.]